Faith Works

Ministry Models for a Hurting World

Joyce Sweeney Martin

2782

"Faith and works, works and faith, fit
together hand in glove" (James 2:17 *The Message*).

Woman's Missionary Union
Birmingham, Alabama

Woman's Missionary Union
P. O. Box 830010
Birmingham, AL 35283-0010

Dewey Decimal Classification: 261.8
Subject Headings: CHURCH AND SOCIAL PROBLEMS
                          CHURCH WORK
                          MISSIONS, CHRISTIAN
                          AIDS (DISEASE)
                          HOMELESSNESS
                          ABORTION
                          LITERACY
                          HUNGER
                          GAMBLING

Cover design by Kelly Schultz

ISBN: 1-56309-173-9
W964146•0896•5M1

Contents

Introduction vii

Chapter 1: Caring for Persons with AIDS 1

Chapter 2: Sheltering the Homeless 27

Chapter 3: Valuing Life 51

Chapter 4: Teaching Others to Read 77

Chapter 5: Feeding the Hungry 101

Chapter 6: Unmasking Gambling 121

Epilogue 141

"Faith and works,
works and faith,
fit together hand in glove. . . .
'I'm telling the solemn truth: Whenever you did one of
these things to someone overlooked or ignored, that was
me—you did it to me'"
(James 2:17; Matt. 25:40 *The Message*).

Foreword

This is a book about courage—the courage of people and churches who shifted emphasis from themselves to other people. It takes courage to be an "other carer," and this book tells about much caring.

I have always believed three things about how the church ministers to other people.

First, it is a privilege for the church to minister. The community shows much respect for the church when it allows the church to minister. Actually, individuals and churches earn the right to minister to others. We have in *Faith Works* models of churches that have earned the right.

Second, ministry is person-centered; and in that sense, love is made visible. *Faith Works* speaks to many needs—both physical and spiritual hunger, freedom for the spirit, education, and a safe and accepting home. Ministry speaks to human and spiritual needs. It is love made visible. It is people-oriented. It is being Jesus.

Third, ministry is giving with no strings attached. Throughout *Faith Works,* people minister in the name of Christ because of a personal need, without requiring a response from the person being ministered to. There is no room in ministry for, "You may have this if . . ." or "I will do that for you if . . ." Ministry means we make the first move, not expecting a second move from the other person. We take the initiative in reaching out. This is the Jesus way.

Faith Works is a book for certain needs. Joyce Sweeney Martin not only shares what others are doing but also makes it possible for you to believe you can do these things.

There is much to choose from that will meet the need in your setting.

Don Hammonds
Interim Vice-President, Ministry Section
Home Mission Board

Introduction

"Faith and works,
works and faith,
fit together hand in glove. . . .
'I'm telling the solemn truth: Whenever you did one of these things to someone overlooked or ignored, that was me—you did it to me'"
(James 2:17; Matt. 25:40 *The Message).*

AIDS . . . homelessness . . . crisis pregnancy . . . hunger . . . illiteracy . . . gambling. These are just the tip of the iceberg in a hurting world.

I've felt the pain in the touch of a young woman facing death from AIDS and seen the fear in the eyes of a teenaged girl facing an unwanted pregnancy. I've sensed the utter hopelessness in the demeanor of a homeless man and the listlessness of a hungry child. I've heard the embarrassment in the voice of a senior adult trying to hide his inability to read and write. I know I'm rarely more than a hand away from a hurting world.

But I, like many Christians, am easily overwhelmed by the great number of hurting people and the scope of the hurts in the world. Each problem seems to have its own tangled issues, its own complexities, its own questions. Frankly, sometimes I would prefer to give up.

Just when I'm ready to give in to despair—or to a comfortable life—God sends some of His choice servants into my life to get me back on track. He sends fellow believers who model a faith that really works in a hurting world.

In this book, I'd like to introduce you to some of these Christians and the ministries in which they are involved. Some of these people I have known personally for many years; most I have met recently through the recommendations of friends. Some of their ministry stories I have seen firsthand; most I have encountered via telephone and fax machine. They represent many Christian groups: Baptist; Presbyterian; Roman Catholic; Methodist; Church of Christ—to name a few. They are spread from California to Massachusetts, Illinois to Florida.

In *Faith Works,* you will meet:

•Christians with a passion for God and a passion for people

•Christians who take seriously their role as models of a faith that works in a hurting world

•Christians for whom ministry is not an option, but a necessity. They don't let difficult questions with debatable answers deter them from ministering in Jesus' name

•Christians who are intentional and responsible in addressing the needs of a hurting world

•Christians who balance compassion with common sense, mercy with truth.

In *Faith Works,* you will encounter ministry models developed as a result of these Christians walking their faith into a hurting world. These ministries include:

•AIDS ministries in Alabama and North Carolina

•Homeless ministries in California, Kentucky, and Florida

•Crisis pregnancy ministries in Oklahoma, Florida, Texas, Illinois, and South Carolina

•Literacy missions ministries in Georgia, New York, and California

•Hunger/economic development ministries in Missouri and Massachusetts

In *Faith Works,* you will read about the explosive growth of gambling across the nation.

And in *Faith Works,* you will learn specific how-tos so you can follow these models and walk your faith into your world.

Only with the encouragement and support of Larry, my husband and best friend, could I have seen this book become reality. To Larry, who in our 31 years of marriage has modeled a faith that works up close and personal as well as a faith that works in ministry to a hurting world, I dedicate this book.

Joyce Sweeney Martin
February 1996

The Night AIDS Came to Church

No street lights shone in this part of rural Alabama where I recently spoke one evening. The event was sponsored by the Woman's Missionary Union (WMU), a missions arm of most Southern Baptist churches.

Basic information about HIV/AIDS was shared. A young man told his powerful, personal story of what it is like to live with HIV, and the people were challenged to respond in a compassionate, loving way. And then it happened.

The *leader* of the WMU, a single mom, stood and thanked everyone for coming, and said, "There is something I want to share with you. This subject is near to my heart. You see, I am HIV positive, and so is my little boy."

And now that congregation knows what is true for every congregation in Alabama. We too have a church member or relative with AIDS. Thank God now one more feels safe enough to tell others.[1]

> Malcolm Marler
> Director, AIDS Education and Ministry Project
> Birmingham, Alabama

"Search your heart and do what Jesus would do."—Charles Reed

1

Caring for Persons with AIDS

J ust give me a call when he's dead.' Stunned, I hung up the phone in bewilderment that a father could respond so coldly to the news that his son was dying of AIDS.

"As the assistant director of a homeless shelter [in Savannah, Ga.], I discovered there was no one and no place to care for Richard during the last stage of his life. Richard had been found living in an abandoned building, and having no family willing to care for him, the last resort was a homeless shelter.

"For the next month, workers at [Grace House] spent their time haphazardly caring for Richard. I tried desperately to find some answers to the situation. Why was there no place for Richard? Where was the church? Where were family and friends?"[2]

The withdrawal of family members and friends. The confusion of people who want to help. The refusal of those who don't. The ostrichlike response of the church. In three short paragraphs, Dianne Fuller captured the anguish of the disease that won't go away.

Since acquired immune deficiency syndrome (AIDS) burst onto the scene in 1980, more than 1 million people have died of the disease worldwide. An estimated 18 million adults and 1.5 million children around the world have been infected with the human immunodeficiency virus

(HIV), which causes AIDS. And the AIDS epidemic continues to spread. In 1994 alone, the number of AIDS cases worldwide rose by 20 percent.[3] Half of all HIV-positive people develop AIDS within nine years of contracting the virus, and 40 percent die within that period.[4]

On the world scene:

•Every 7 minutes someone dies of AIDS.

•Every 24 hours 8,000 new persons become infected.

•About 75 percent of the people who are HIV-positive were infected through heterosexual activity.[5]

•Nearly half of all new AIDS patients are women.[6]

In the United States, from the time the first case of the mysterious new immune system disorder was documented in June 1981 to June 1982, only about 400 cases of AIDS were reported in the entire country.[7] But by the end of June 1995, that number had grown to nearly a half million (476,899).[8] At least 1 million more had been infected with HIV.[9] By 1995, 1 out of every 250 Americans was infected with HIV; and more than 270,000 had died from AIDS—more than died in the last three US wars combined.[10]

In the United States:

•AIDS is now the leading cause of death among all Americans aged 25 to 44.[11]

•One in every 92 American men aged 27 to 39 may be battling the AIDS virus.[12]

•Heterosexual women in childbearing years now comprise the fastest growing group of new HIV/AIDS cases. AIDS is no longer primarily a gay disease.[13]

•About 25 percent of mothers with the HIV virus infect their babies.[14]

Even though the government reported in late 1995 that AIDS appeared to be leveling off with 40,000 new infections every year balanced by about 40,000 deaths, AIDS experts at the Centers for Disease Control and Prevention (CDC) in Atlanta warn this is just an illusion. CDC researchers say the numbers have not changed much since 1993 because it takes so long for the virus to kill. And while there has been a drop in new infections in Anglo men in recent years, the risk for young minorities and women has increased.[15]

While there is still no medical cure in sight, hardly a week goes by without an announcement of some advance on the AIDS front.[16] One of the most promising moments came in February 1996 when word came of a new class of drugs called *protease inhibitors* which seem to change the course of the disease, delaying both symptoms and death.[17]

In many quarters, fear, intolerance, and ignorance have accompanied the rise in HIV/AIDS. Children with AIDS have been barred from school classrooms and from church facilities. Family members have abandoned their loved ones to die lonely and frightening deaths. Instead of being encircled with warmth and care, many people with HIV/AIDS have been left to struggle alone, encased in secrecy.

Even as late as 1990, it was possible for Christians to stay relatively detached from the crisis. Fred and Lavada Loper, Southern Baptist national medical missionaries, recall the curious looks they often received as they began crisscrossing the country speaking about AIDS. Many Christians and their churches responded in silence either because they did not know what to do or say or because they thought AIDS would go away. Others responded with judgment and condemnation. But that has changed profoundly over the last six years, the Lopers say.

"Now, whether we are speaking in a church in the most rural area of Mississippi or the most crowded city blocks of New York City, HIV infection and AIDS is already there," says Fred Loper.[18] As the disease has moved closer to home, and as AIDS has a face in more communities and churches, Christians individually and collectively are choosing a faith response.

Thankfully, pioneers like the Lopers of Oklahoma City, Charles Reed in Shelby, North Carolina, and Malcolm Marler in Birmingham, Alabama, provide models of a faith that works even in the midst of a crisis as devastating as AIDS. "Long ago, Jesus taught us that ministering to the needs of others is always a messy business," Fred Loper says. "But He never failed to love and to help. We need to imitate Him."[19]

Love with No Conditions

"Someone who loves you very much called and asked me to visit you," Charles Reed told the gaunt young man lying in the hospital bed.

"I know who called you," the young man replied. "That woman has shown me more love than anyone I have ever known."

Jim (not his real name) was in the last stages of AIDS. He was miles away from his family—estranged and alone. And yet, when his ex-mother-in-law heard about his illness, she had made the long trip from Oklahoma to North Carolina to bring his little daughter to see her father one last time. In the course of the visit, Jim had asked to see a local Baptist minister. His ex-mother-in-law called Charles Reed.

Jim was in his early 40s. Once, he had been a healthy 240-pound young man. Now, he was little more than an emaciated pile of bones. But in that pile of bones beat the heart of a man who wanted to make things right with God.

"After telling me about living with AIDS and about his estrangement from family and friends, Jim went on to say he was living proof that 'the wages of sin is death,'" Charles remembers. That's what Jim wanted to tell a preacher from the same faith tradition he had known in his youth.

Still, there was more Jim wanted to say.

"But I want you to know I know the rest of that verse," Jim said, quoting Romans 6:23. "'The gift of God is eternal life in Christ Jesus our Lord.'"

That was Jim's deathbed confession. Two days later, with Charles at his side, Jim died.

The Questions

Those few days of ministry to Jim were filled with defining moments for Charles.

•Moments with fears about how AIDS is transmitted, fears about his personal safety.

"I remember my questions as I made my way to Jim's room. Will I get AIDS by going to his room? What will happen if we shake hands? I didn't even anticipate Jim's tears which would fall on my hands," Charles says.

Then the nurse who helped Charles gown and mask up—not to protect Charles from Jim, but to keep Jim from getting any germs Charles might carry in—put his mind at ease.

"You won't catch the disease by talk," she said.

•Moments with questions about what word from God he, as an ordained minister, should offer.

Jim soon put that worry to rest.

"He didn't need my sermon, condemnation, or judgment. He needed a listening ear and compassion to hear his last words," Charles says.

•Moments which would define Charles's future ministry to AIDS patients as sometimes simply presence and nothing more; or praying with a person with AIDS (PWA) and family members when they are scared to call anyone from their church.

That day in 1985 was the first of many days Charles has spent with PWAs.

"Until then, I didn't know much about the disease, but after hearing Jim's story of social isolation which he said was worse than his physical suffering, I knew I needed to go to PWAs and not run from people in need," Charles says.

From his brief encounter with Jim, Charles learned that Jim's "totality as a person was a lot more than the disease that took his life, a lot more even than how he contracted the disease." Charles came to understand that "God loved Jim and sent his Son to die for him just as much as for me."

As Charles began to process some of his questions about AIDS and to consider what a Christian's response should be, he kept asking himself, "What would Jesus do?"

He found his answer in Charles Sheldon's classic *In His Steps.* "Jesus would get involved."

The Response

In the years immediately after Jim's death, Charles had a few opportunities to minister to PWAs and their families. Then, as AIDS began to appear in more churches and communities of North Carolina in the early 1990s, he began the second phase of his ministry. He began helping pastors and laypeople learn about AIDS.

In 1992, Charles surveyed the pastors in Kings Mountain Baptist Association with which he works to determine what help they needed in addressing the growing AIDS epidemic. With their responses in hand, he designed a seminar called "When AIDS Has a Face in Your Church."

One hundred twenty-seven laypeople, clergy, and health professionals registered for the seminar to hear experts in AIDS research and patient care. An epidemiologist talked about the medical aspects of AIDS. An HIV-positive social worker who once was an ordained Southern Baptist minister talked about her personal journey. The nun/director of a Roman Catholic AIDS hospice talked about how to minister to AIDS patients and their loved ones. A Church of God husband and wife ministry team shared how their church stood beside them when they lost their son to AIDS.

"That was the starting point," Charles says. "The conference opened up the opportunity for me to go into churches to speak and to present basic AIDS education programs for youth and adults."

In the years since, Charles has been instrumental in helping the North Carolina Baptist Convention provide AIDS information to all the churches in the convention.

We Have AIDS at Our House

In Her Own Words: One Mother's Story
by Nancy Miller

Nancy Miller is an AIDS educator and mother of a son who died with AIDS.

"We spent every minute of the last month of Stephen's life caring for him, our youngest child. He was just twenty-six years old. His life had been exciting to him and to us, his family. The last twenty months had been a time of wrestling with a disease we could not chart. The yo-yo effect had taken its toll on our emotions. High hopes were viciously dashed by the reality of a new problem, a fever, a rash, and/or Pneumocystis pneumonia. New medical and legal personalities and governmental forms required hard-earned patience. The medical language for AIDS was a difficult learning experience. The social stigma was suffocating."[20]

"If only the congregation could say the "A" word. . . . How we yearned to feel free to raise our hands in prayer meeting and ask for prayer for Stephen and each of our family members. It could only have been done had we been assured of support and love. Understanding would have been nice, too, but that may have asked for too much. How could one understand another's dilemma unless it has been experienced? We felt claustrophobic, afraid, and betrayed."[21]

"I remember applying for public assistance for Stephen. Like most people, we never thought that would be something we would ever have to do. How wonderful it would have been to have someone to go with me."[22]

"As the disease progresses, families find daily tasks and decisions increasingly difficult. In the last five months of Stephen's life, he lost his sight, hearing, and ability to walk without braces. Shingles were outside and inside his body. The virus entered his spinal column and traveled to his brain. Thrush sometimes made it virtually impossible for him to swallow. Food had no taste due to the virus and medications. We watched Stephen's weight fall from one hundred forty-five pounds to sixty-five pounds at the time of his death. Until dementia conquered his brain, he knew his body was dying. He watched the deterioration with an unbelievably optimistic attitude. When told he had three weeks left to live, he said, 'I am not afraid to die. The Lord and I have taken care of that. But I do dread the process.' He had every right to do just that.

"The point is that the family becomes weary. Without the warmth and help of others who will enter their pain, the journey is too arduous to bear. Even now, some four years later, we feel the effects. . . .

"In the early days of AIDS in our family, we kept the condition to ourselves. One by one, we trusted a friend or co-worker with our story."[23]

"When our son, Stephen, was fifteen months into his diagnosis, he was in school, maintaining a 3.8 grade point average. It was Christmas, and his spirits were high. He saw himself as an achiever and was excited about his decision for his major and thoroughly enjoyed his studies. Within five weeks his sight was gone. His hopes and dreams were dashed. No longer did he demonstrate a positive sense of personhood or a feeling of control of his life. Someone, without our knowing, contacted the library to send Stephen a tape player and tapes of music and stories to his liking. . . .

"Someone else notified the Center for Independent Living of his condition. They brought Stephen a watch which voiced the time. They taught him to walk with a cane. He learned to work on a computer for the seeing impaired. He was still somebody! He realized he could maintain quality, control and dignity in his life.

"A bit later we made a trip to Florida and Jerry, Stephen's friend, went with us. Jerry took time off work to offer his presence to Stephen. Friend to friend, they could share and give to each other memories to last a lifetime. We call that a special gift."[24]

"One day Marilyn phoned asking if she could bring lunch. Though we were thankful for the food, it was not an unusual offering. We had not extended dinner invitations for fear guests would not come or that they would be anxious. After all, we had AIDS at our house. Marilyn came and put the food on the table. What a lovely meal. Stephen thanked her, 'The food is wonderful,' he said, 'but I thank you most of all for eating it with us.' She had gone the extra mile gracing us with her presence! The power of that experience will stay with us forever.

"You must know about the calendar. Stephen had come home from the hospital for the last time. He had to be fed with a dropper, diapered, bathed, hugged, talked to, and massaged. He relied on total care. A group of friends put together a month's calendar with squares in which the friends could write their names, phone numbers, time they could stay, and what they would do while they were with us. We were given the control of the offering. They did not insist, nor did they feel rejected if we did not need them at that particular time. Sometimes one could stay for fifteen minutes. Others would bring food, wash clothes, or sit beside Stephen while we went for a walk. . . .

"A young woman came for thirty minutes. She sat with Stephen while Chip and I walked. When she left we found a poem at the foot of his bed. We read it to his unhearing ears and to our broken hearts. It was a poem offering tribute to the young man who had befriended her and now she was losing. We have not seen her since, but the gift was very special to us and gave us strength.

"Michael came to tell us he had a new car and would like us to ride in it. He knew we did not care about his new car at the time, but he also knew we needed to leave the house for refreshment. He produced a sitter, Claressa, and compelled us to go with him. Having been gone for about fifteen minutes, we returned to hear the most beautiful melody coming from our house. Claressa was singing. So beautiful was the sound, so lovely were the lyrics, she sang the song again for Stephen's memorial service. The inspiration of such a beautiful gift has lifted us many times.

"Quinn said he did not have to work that night. Could he come and stay with Stephen so we could go to bed for the first time in three weeks? We accepted his gift and we prepared for him a bed about twenty feet away from Stephen's hospice bed. Early in the morning I entered Stephen's room to find Quinn on the floor immediately beside Stephen's bed. In answer to my question, 'Why?' he said, 'I do not like the way he is breathing and I did not want him to die alone.' We call that a 'God' gift.

"It was the same group of friends who brought me a dozen roses for Mother's Day. They did what they knew Stephen would do if he were conscious and well.

"Another intimate group of our friends came to our side that late May morning. They surrounded us literally with their arms as Chip and I stood on each side of Stephen's bed and held his hands. It was a sacred time and together we witnessed Stephen's homegoing."[25]

Grace with No Strings

Malcolm Marler once longed to go to India to work with Mother Teresa. Then, he explains, "Suddenly it clicked that I could reach out to the dying in my own backyard, that AIDS patients are the lepers of today and need my help."

So in March 1994, Malcolm eagerly accepted an offer to become the first full-time AIDS chaplain at the 1917 Clinic at the University of Alabama at Birmingham (UAB). Now, he works with AIDS outpatients at the clinic which is a part of the UAB School of Medicine. He is director of the AIDS Education and Ministry Project.

For Malcolm, AIDS is the defining issue in our time for people of faith. "If we can't get this right, we can't get a lot of other things right," he says. He agrees with Mother Teresa that "this epidemic will give the Christian Church a challenge to be the compassionate body of Christ."[26]

"The bottom line in approaching AIDS is a person's concept of grace," Malcolm says. "Is it unconditional and a gift for anyone," or are there strings attached?

Malcolm finds a clear model for his work in the life of Jesus. "Flip the pages of the Gospels and point to any story of Jesus and there you will find a guide to any ministry, including AIDS," he says.

Since he became chaplain in March 1994, Malcolm has sought not only to minister to AIDS patients, but also to teach Alabama churches and synagogues how to be havens of compassion for AIDS patients and their loved ones. To accomplish these goals, he has developed a three-pronged interfaith HIV/AIDS ministry:

•GRACE, a first step for clergy and laypeople to learn about HIV/AIDS and how they can make a difference in the epidemic.

•AIDS Care Teams (ACT), a group of 12 or more people who provide unconditional, compassionate care for people with HIV/AIDS and their loved ones.

•Train the Trainers, quarterly all-day training sessions to teach leaders from congregations across Alabama and the Southeast how to develop GRACE and AIDS Care Team programs in their communities.

GRACE (Giving and Receiving AIDS Compassionate Education)

The genesis of GRACE is in itself unique. Michael Saag, founder of the UAB 1917 Clinic, was the first to have a vision for an HIV/AIDS community education program targeting the religious community. While speaking to a Rotary Club meeting in the spring of 1993, the Jewish physician challenged his audience to get involved in HIV preventive education. Ed Dixon, a Birmingham business-man and active Methodist layman, was in the audience that day. Dixon, whose foundation provides funds for continuing education for clergy, called Saag the next week and offered his help.

A year later, Saag hired Malcolm Marler, a Baptist pastor/educator/pastoral counselor as chaplain of the UAB 1917 Clinic.

And so, as Malcolm likes to say, "A Jewish physician and a Methodist layman convinced a state university hospital to hire a Baptist to develop an interfaith outreach program" to educate churches and synagogues about AIDS.

Shortly after coming to the clinic, Malcolm began GRACE as a first step for clergy and laypeople to learn the facts about HIV/AIDS and to learn how they could make a difference in the lives of those affected by the disease.

Every Friday morning, a new group of volunteers meet for two hours at the UAB 1917 Clinic. In the first year and three months, almost 600 people attended.

Each week the program has three components:

•FACTS—HIV/AIDS information presented by a medical team member, followed by time for questions from GRACE group members

•FACES—The human side as told by a person living with HIV/AIDS or by a family member

•FAITH response—Discussion of a variety of individual and congregational responses that can make a difference in the lives of people affected by HIV/AIDS.

AIDS Care Teams (ACT)

After several people who had attended a GRACE group expressed interest in getting more involved in AIDS education and ministry, Joe Elmore, a retired Methodist pastor, joined the staff on a part-time basis to develop AIDS Care Teams.

AIDS Care Teams are designed to create family for AIDS patients and their caregivers by providing them with practical, emotional, and spiritual support.

The first teams began their ministry in January 1995. The approach caught on quickly in places of worship around Alabama. By January 1996, more than 40 AIDS Care Teams had been recruited, trained, and activated in nine cities and towns across Alabama. These Care Teams include more than 500 people from Baptist, Catholic, Episcopal, Jewish, Lutheran, Methodist, Metropolitan Community, and Presbyterian congregations. In addition, hospital employees and clinic volunteers, university students, an AIDS service organization, a community nonprofit organization, and the staff of a religious denomination have also formed Care Teams.

Anglo teams from suburban congregations care for inner-city patients. A Jewish team works with Baptist AIDS patients. Inner-city African Americans minister to people of a different skin color. Teams of one faith group minister to people of other faith groups.

Each new AIDS Care Team which forms is trained at the UAB 1917 Clinic. The training is cosponsored by nine Birmingham AIDS agencies and clinics.

Train the Trainers

Once a quarter, the UAB 1917 Clinic offers an all-day training session for congregational leaders who want to develop GRACE groups and AIDS Care Teams in their communities. Eventually, Malcolm hopes to set up a training center at the clinic where people from across Alabama and the Southeast could come for intensive training.

Malcolm also publishes a quarterly newsletter called "Red Ribbon Reflections" as a way to tie all the AIDS ministries together and to offer encouragement and support to the people involved in AIDS ministries. By late 1995, more than 1,700 people who had expressed a serious interest in HIV/AIDS ministry were on the mailing list.

Faith with Feet
In His Own Words: Diary of a Volunteer

On the day he met Dick, a 33-year-old AIDS patient, Manly Yeilding began a four-month journey unlike any he had known before. It was an experience which would teach him "what care and love, expecting nothing in return, really is," Manly says. That day, February 16, 1995, Manly took his first steps as a member of the first AIDS Care Team formed by Canterbury United Methodist Church in Birmingham, Alabama.

Below, in his own words, are excerpts from the 65-year-old attorney's diary:

Thursday, February 16. 1995
Dick was waiting with Jim, his friend, at 7:50 A.M. on a rainy Thursday morning when I drove up . . . to meet him for the first time. An 8:00 A.M. appointment with the ophthalmologist was our destination. . . .

Our short drive was consumed mainly with Dick's directions to the doctor's office. His soft-spoken, polite demeanor made our introduction to each other easy. . . .

My main concern about the first visit centered around whether I would have time or willingness to offer to go out for coffee and a sweet roll before returning to Dick's condo. I resolved my question by remembering my 10:00 o'clock office appointment and some insecurity about how much more involvement I or Dick wanted on the first meeting.

I only hope that Dick found me to be as real and caring as I found him. Did I feel awkward? A little, but only of my own making.

Thursday, March 30, 1995
[Another visit to the clinic.] Because I had a 10:00 [o'clock] appointment at the office, we didn't stop for coffee as I had mentioned on Tuesday. I still have ambiguous feelings about being much more than a chauffeur.

Monday, April 3, 1995
Dick has "perked up" since the team got involved. . . . Janice [another Care Team member] signed off on a phone conversation one night, "Have sweet dreams," and Dick broke up. He told Ann [another member] the next day that was the nicest thing anybody had said.

Thursday, April 27, 1995
Dick asked me about my field of practice and I got some info to do a will for him.

Monday, June 5, 1995
Regular Care Team meeting. [Dick's mother was present.] Dick was put into the hospital today. [His mother] was so appreciative of the Care Team and prayed a moving prayer at the end of the session. To be in the presence of such a loving mother who lives with such heartache brought many twinges and chill bumps. . . . In her prayer, [she] said that love is what anyone needs most when sick for any reason— particularly sick with AIDS which is looked so down on.

Wednesday, June 21, 1995
[The hospital took Dick off all medicine] and sent him home to die.

Thursday, June 22, 1995
I had a nice 45-minute visit with Dick. He was in bed. . . . He carefully reread the [will] before signing it in the presence of the three of us. Before leaving, I asked if there was anything I could bring him that might taste good. He mentioned cantaloupe. . . .

   [That night] I stopped [back] by Dick's to leave the fruit. . . . Dick was lying on the sofa. . . . I told Fred that Susan (not her real name) [a friend of Dick's at the farmer's market] wanted me to give him a hug [for her] which pleased him and which I did. (I had left him in tears in the afternoon, realizing as I left that a hug or touch of any kind was the thing to do, and I didn't. Susan gave me another chance.) I returned to the car and on home, knowing that the last 24 hours had been filled with some of life's richest blessings—real experiences of love and caring about others.

Sunday, June 25, 1995
After lunch at home, I carried a tray of goodies to Dick. . . . All of [his] family [including a missionary brother] had

been here at some point during the weekend. . . . My impression is that the brothers have bid their final farewell to each other. The missionary brother had brought his guitar and got in a nice session with Dick. Apparently, Dick has let it be known he wants no religious "stuff" and the family is honoring his wishes.

Friday, June 30, 1995
Friday was Dick's birthday (34) and I stopped by with a cake and some bread. . . . Dick appeared to be close to "the end." . . . I was very moved by this short visit which I was afraid was probably my last with Dick. . . .

The meaning of life and death seem confused as I begin another week—closely related and yet far apart.

Monday, July 17, 1995
Dick is confined to the bed. . . . I stopped by. (He is ambivalent about being terminal—doesn't really want to believe it. . . .) He was worried that visits from the Care Team may be waning.

[Later] Dick's nausea did not "overcome" me, but I was glad that John was there to help him. I don't think I could handle that—know I would not want to try.

I've talked to several of the Canterbury folks trying to spread our visits through the week.

Saturday, July 22, 1995
Early yesterday, I took some peaches and tomatoes. . . . Sat with Dick about ten minutes. His eyes were glazed and he was shaking (but not cold). He was more subdued than most any other time—but rational and aware. . . . I felt him (through the cover) and he is very bony. I'll be relieved when he takes his last breath (for some reason it is hard to write "when he dies").

Monday, July 24, 1995
I stopped by for about an hour in the late afternoon. . . .
Dick was awake, but [not] up to a visit. . . . That was the
first time he had declined a visit. . . .

I really wanted to go in and sit with Dick, but didn't
think I should ask.

Wednesday, July 26, 1995
I visited at the condo. . . . Dick appeared comfortable, but
just "hanging on."

Thursday, July 27, 1995
I got a call . . . about 10:15 saying that Dick had died at
5:00 A.M. . . . I stopped by the condo about 1:15.

Friday, July 28, 1995
This morning, I met with [Dick's parents] at my office and
went over the will and the waivers.

Sunday, July 30, 1995
Arriving early for the 3:00 service [in the Canterbury
chapel], I found [Dick's parents] already [there]. . . . Someone had planned for the family and the Care Team members to wear boutonnieres and [Dick's mother] had a
corsage. . . . [In the service someone told about the previous Easter when Dick and his friend] visited Canterbury
and sat on the back row. . . . (The next time they were at
the church was on [the associate pastor's] last Sunday [he
was a Care Team member], and they sat on the first pew.)

(All names, except Manly Yeilding's, have been changed.)

Put Your Faith to Work

**If you want to minister to persons with AIDS (PWAs)
either through a group or on your own, take the following
steps.**

•First, deal with your fears about AIDS. Take advantage of seminars, books, and discussion groups to deal with your fears and to learn about HIV/AIDS. Study the life of Jesus; ask what He would do.

•Conduct a community needs assessment. Contact community agencies to learn how many people in your community are affected by AIDS. Ask about organizations currently assisting persons with AIDS and their loved ones. Ask yourself: What is being done to minister to these people in the name of Christ? What must I do?

•Get training. Training should include: AIDS/HIV education, how to care for the sick (including universal precautions for working with AIDS patients), active listening and communication skills, grief counseling, do's and don'ts of ministry, and how to discuss spiritual issues with a PWA.

Find out about training in your area offered through churches involved in AIDS ministries, the public health department, the American Red Cross, your local denominational office, or other AIDS ministries.

If you minister as a part of a group, take the following steps.

•Start an AIDS Care Team in your congregation. Before you begin, find out if your congregation is open to AIDS ministries. If not, be a loving advocate in your congregation for AIDS awareness/education and concern.

•Volunteer at a local AIDS organization or at a medical facility that treats AIDS patients. Call the health department, Red Cross, or your congregation's denominational headquarters for a list. Be sure you can work within the philosophy of the agency before signing on as a volunteer.

•Start a support group for AIDS patients.

•Start a support group for AIDS caregivers.

•Start a support group for people who have lost relatives or friends to AIDS.

If you minister solo, take the following steps.

(These ideas require minimal time involvement and may serve as entry points or as onetime ministry projects for ministry to PWAs and their loved ones.)

•Provide a PWA transportation to the doctor.

•Be an advocate for a PWA with insurance companies, social service agencies, and medical personnel.

•Be a phone buddy for a caregiver. Provide a listening ear and a sympathetic heart.

•Provide respite (rest) care for a caregiver. Sit with the loved one while the caregiver takes a break.

•"Adopt" a child of a PWA. Spend time together. Talk, help with homework, or go to the movies.

•Minister to PWAs in the same way you would to anyone with a life-threatening illness: provide food; run errands; etc.

•Become an AIDS advocate (see p. 21 for how to be an effective advocate).

Selected Resources for HIV/AIDS Ministry

The following resources offer specific, detailed help on how to get started in ministry to PWAs and their loved ones.

Books, Booklets
Amos, William E. Jr. *When AIDS Comes to Church.* Philadelphia: Westminster Press, 1988.

Anderson, Monnie. *Ideas for Hospital Ministries.* Birmingham, AL: New Hope, 1992.

Centers for Disease Control National AIDS Clearinghouse, 1 (800) 458-5231. Offers an array of helpful resources.

Cummings, Margaret Ann. *Touched by AIDS.* Birmingham, AL: World Changers Resources, 1992. A booklet to help youth know how to help a person with AIDS or how to help the family of an AIDS patient.

Marler, Malcolm. *Ideas for Homebound Ministries.* Birmingham, AL: New Hope, 1993.

Sunderland, Ronald H., and Earl E. Shelp. *Handle with Care: A Handbook for Care Teams Serving People with AIDS.* Nashville: Abingdon Press, 1990.

Videos and Tapes
Talking with Teens. San Francisco AIDS Foundation (P. O. Box 6182, San Francisco, CA 94101; $65.00). May be found in some public libraries, community organizations, or video stores.

Washington AIDS Conference (three tapes). National Association of Evangelicals (P. O. Box 28, Wheaton, IL 60189; $15.00).

Computer Services
Computerized AIDS Ministries Resource Network (CAM) is a bulletin board service of the United Methodist Church that links people engaged in HIV/AIDS ministries. Dial 1 (212) 222-2135 through your personal computer and modem.

•AIDS Information Ministries, P. O. Box 136116, Fort Worth, TX 76136.
•Christian AIDS Services Alliance, P. O. Box 23277, Washington, DC 20026.
•Christian AIDS Network, 1411 N. Classen Boulevard, Suite 111, Oklahoma City, OK 73106.
•AIDS Education and Ministry Project, UAB 1917 Clinic, 908 South 20th Street, Birmingham, AL 35294-2050; phone: (205) 975-9129; fax: (205) 975-6448;
E-mail: Malcolm@Byrd1917@his.uab.edu

How to Be an Effective Advocate
•Propose solutions to the problems being addressed.
•Propose solutions which empower those needing help to make decisions about their own lives.
•Develop partnerships inside the human systems they are trying to influence.
•Use more than one approach.

Source: Diana Garland, *Precious in His Sight* (A Guide to Child Advocacy), 2d ed. (Birmingham, AL: New Hope, 1996), 146–48.

AIDS: A Chronology

June 5, 1981—The first cases of a mysterious immune system disorder are documented in the United States. The Centers for Disease Control and Prevention (CDC) cites the cases of five homosexual men in Los Angeles with pneumocystis carinii, a rare form of pneumonia. The disease is later found to be one of many opportunistic infections that occurs in people with AIDS. Most of the early reported cases in the US occur in gay men.

July 27, 1982—The CDC names the new disease AIDS (acquired immune deficiency syndrome).

April 1984—Scientists in France and the United States announce simultaneously that they have isolated the virus that causes AIDS, later named the human immunodeficiency virus (HIV).

March 1985—The first blood test to detect the presence of antibodies to HIV is approved for use in the United States. To prevent the further spread of AIDS through transfusions of tainted blood, US blood banks introduce blood-screening tests.

1987—AZTS (zidovudine) is the first drug to receive Food and Drug Administration (FDA) approval for treatment of AIDS.

1988—By August, the number of AIDS cases in the US reaches 100,000.

1991—By November, the number of AIDS cases in the US reaches 200,000, having doubled in just over two years.

February 1995—The CDC reports that AIDS has become the leading cause of death among all Americans aged 25 to 44.

Source: *Congressional Quarterly Researcher,* April 21, 1995.

AIDS Facts

HIV is not spread through:
- coughing, sneezing
- mosquitoes, fleas
- donating blood
- worshiping with a person
- sharing a meal
- playing in the nursery with a child who has HIV/AIDS
- touching, shaking hands, hugging, kissing
- using same rest rooms or drinking fountains
- visiting the home or hospital room of a person with HIV/AIDS
- drying the tears of someone with HIV/AIDS

HIV is spread through:
- having unprotected sex (including oral sex) with someone who is HIV-infected
- sharing needles or syringes with someone who is infected
- from an infected mother to her baby during pregnancy or childbirth, and rarely, through breast-feeding

For Bible Study

Our works and our faith—both come from our understanding of God as expressed in the Bible. Use these passages to enhance your understanding of how and why we minister to people touched by AIDS.

Mark 1:40–45   Luke 10:25–37

Luke 5:12–16   Matthew 25:31–46

Luke 6:37–42

Notes

[1] Malcolm Marler, "The Night AIDS Came to the WMU," *Red Ribbon Reflections,* October-November-December 1995, 4.

[2] Dianne R. Fuller, "Church's Compassion Can Fill Isolation of People with AIDS," *Baptists Today,* October 19, 1995, 6.

[3] Mary H. Cooper, "Combating AIDS: The Issues," *Congressional Quarterly Researcher,* April 21, 1995, 347.

[4] Geoffrey Cowley, "Living Longer with HIV," *Newsweek,* February 12, 1996, 60.

[5] Malcolm Marler, "Current Trends," *GRACE,* September 27, 1995, 6.

[6] "The Changing Stats on AIDS," *Current Health,* November 1993, 12.

[7] Ibid.

[8] June 1995 Report (Atlanta, GA: Centers for Disease Control and Prevention).

[9] "The Changing Stats on AIDS," 12.

[10] Marler, "Current Trends," 6.

[11] Lauran Neergaard, "AIDS Virus Found High in Young Men," *Louisville (Ky.) Courier-Journal,* November 24, 1995.

[12] Ibid.

[13] Marler, "Current Trends," 6.

[14] Lauran Neergaard, "Doctors Would Withhold Care of HIV Babies, Study Finds," *Louisville (Ky.) Courier-Journal,* November 13, 1995.

[15] Neergaard, "AIDS Virus Found High in Young Men."

[16] Christine Gorman, "Battling the AIDS Virus," *Time,* February 12, 1996, 62.

24

[17]Cowley, "Living Longer with AIDS," 60.

[18]Fred Loper, "This Trail of Tears Leads to Ministry," *MissionsUSA,* January-February 1995, 76.

[19]Ibid.

[20]Nancy Miller, "HIV/AIDS Ministry: Putting a Face to AIDS," *AIDS Resource Packet* (Atlanta: Ethics and Public Policy Ministry Group of the Cooperative Baptist Fellowship, 1994), III:24. Used by permission.

[21]Ibid., III:26.

[22]Ibid.

[23]Ibid., III:26–27.

[24]Ibid., III:27–28.

[25]Ibid., III:28–29.

[26]*Risk the Journey: Kentucky Woman's Missionary Union Project HELP: AIDS Resource Kit* (Louisville: Kentucky Woman's Missionary Union), 4-1.

Day by day.
 A person needs food
  and clothes
   and a roof overhead.
Day by day.
 A person needs love
  and security
   and the feeling that somebody
   cares.
Day by day.
 But what if there isn't
  food enough
   clothes enough?
 But what if there is
  a leaky roof
   or no roof at all?
But what if there is
 no love
  no security
   no one to care?
What's a person to do,
Day by day?

—Joyce Sweeney Martin

"I often tell my people, 'Ministry is inconvenient,' but if Jesus were here, this is what He would be doing."
—Pastor Faith Conklin

2

$\mathcal{S}$heltering the Homeless

It was dubbed a "numerical snapshot" of the homeless in America. On the night of March 20, 1990, surveyors from the US Census Bureau fanned out across the nation, visiting more than 39,000 sites frequented by the homeless. They counted people in places ranging from emergency shelters and homes for abused women to farm dormitories and refuges for runaways. That night the count was 459,209.[1]

While census officials acknowledged the count was only a snapshot of the homeless on one night—not an estimate of the total number of homeless or an actual count—at least it was an attempt to come up with a reliable figure.

But that snapshot not only focused attention on the issue of the homeless count, it also encapsulated other questions which had sprung up in the previous decade: Who are the homeless? Why are they homeless? What are the best ways to help the homeless?

These questions had been churning in the national consciousness for some time. During the 1970s and 1980s, news reports, documentaries, exposés, and books had called Americans to address or at least acknowledge the plight of the increasing numbers of homeless in the inner city, the suburbs, and the countryside. Americans generally were sympathetic to the homeless and were willing to offer financial help. A September 1989 *Washington Post*-ABC Poll found that 71 percent of those surveyed wanted to increase government spending on programs for the homeless, even if it meant higher taxes.[2] Books like *Trevor's Place,* the story of 11-year-old Trevor Ferrell's efforts to help the homeless of Philadelphia, reminded Americans that one person could make a difference.[3]

But somewhere along the way, a shift in attitude occurred. Questions began to surface. By 1990, a controversy was brewing over just how many homeless there really were. One homeless advocacy group reported 2.2 million— or 1 percent of the population as homeless. Other advocacy groups reported even higher numbers.[4]

Granted, experts agree that counting the homeless is difficult, if not impossible. Most homeless individuals move between shelters, single-room occupancy (SRO) hotels, the homes of friends and relatives, and the streets, according to the National Resource Center on Homelessness and Mental Illness.[5] Also, shelters don't have the staff to keep accurate data.

For a nation accustomed to quick solutions, caring turned to cynicism as more and more people questioned the allocation of resources in the face of a situation which did not seem to be improving. Statistics became ideological and political weapons to be manipulated in determining both the scope of homelessness and the consequent expenditure of both government and private sector dollars.

Compassion turned to compassion fatigue. A 1990 *Washington Post*-ABC poll found that only 58 percent would be willing to pay higher taxes to help the homeless, down 13 percent from September 1989.[6]

Debates over the definition of *homeless* sprang up. To the federal government, the homeless are those persons actually living on the street, in shelters, or in some other facility administered expressly for homeless people. To homeless advocates, the homeless include those living in SROs, with family and friends, or in some institution not specifically meant for homeless persons like jails or hospitals.[7]

Contrary to general opinion, there is no typical homeless person. They are a heterogeneous group with a variety of needs. However, four major categories can be identified, according to Carl Resener who has worked with the homeless in Nashville, Tennessee, for more than two decades.

•The Self-Inflicted. The traditional street dweller, the wino, alcoholic, drifter, the loner, and those who have opted out of the "rat race" of life. For the most part, they have chosen to be homeless.

•The Seekers. The displaced people who have lost their jobs and their homes. They have not chosen the streets.

•The Sick and Mentally Ill. Most often they cannot reenter community life without assistance.

•The Stranded. The abused woman, the Vietnam veteran, the runaway/throwaway youth, the ex-offenders, the illegal aliens, the physically and mentally handicapped, and persons with AIDS.[8]

Debates over why people are homeless became commonplace. While three major reasons often are given, even these reasons are disputed.

•Deinstitutionalization of the mentally ill after the passage of the 1963 Community Health Centers Act.

This act deinstitutionalized an estimated 430,000 mentally ill people without providing adequate support systems once the people were mainstreamed into the community. According to advocates for the homeless, in 1963, the population of the country's mental institutions was 505,000; in 1995, it was roughly 125,000. Many people who have been deinstitutionalized now live on the streets.[9]

•Decline in unskilled jobs and low-income housing.

Unskilled day-labor jobs have all but disappeared. And with urban renewal in the 1960s and gentrification (renovation of older housing by upscale home buyers) in the 1970s, many single-room occupancy dwellings disappeared as well.[10]

•Rise in the number of working homeless.

As housing costs rose dramatically in the 1980s, the number of poverty or near-poverty households rose. Also, many low-income people who presently are renters are only a paycheck from homelessness.

Debates over how best to help the homeless intensified. While the focus of help for the homeless in the early 1980s generally centered on providing emergency shelter and emergency assistance, by the late 1980s and early 1990s it had shifted to include long-term solutions as well. Today, classes in budgeting, help with landlord mediation, mental health care, job training, and permanent housing have become a part of the agenda of programs for the homeless. Reflecting this trend, the US Congress passed the Stewart B. McKinney Homeless Assistance Act of July 1987 which provided $490.2 million for emergency shelters, health care, job training, and other related programs. An additional $1.2 billion was allotted during 1988–91. Private groups began to focus on these issues as well.[11]

In the context of this book, two approaches to addressing homelessness merit mention.

•Private nonprofit religious-based organizations which receive government help. These include such well-known groups as Jewish Family Services and Catholic Charities. According to the December 4, 1995, *Time* magazine, 63 percent of Catholic Charities' $1.9 billion 1994 budget came from federal, state, and local governments, including grants from eight different federal agencies.[12] Included in the services provided through Catholic Charities are a number of programs to assist the homeless.

According to the same *Time* article, most other large charities concerned with the poor receive an average of about 31 percent of their total annual budgets from government sources.[13] The Kitchen, Inc., in Kansas City, Missouri, is heavily dependent on government support. Because The Kitchen, Inc., began as a hunger ministry and grew to be a multifaceted ministry, it is modeled in chapter 5 of this book. Many smaller agencies and groups such as Emergency Christian Ministry in Williamsburg, Kentucky, modeled in this chapter receive some government assistance.

•Nonprofit religious-based organizations which do not receive government help.

Services range from soup kitchens to medical and hygiene assistance to temporary housing to support groups to economic development programs. While the Interfaith Cold Weather Shelter in Whittier, California, modeled in this chapter received a onetime government grant and uses food from area food banks, most of the ongoing expenses are covered by member congregations. The community meals program at Metropolitan Baptist Church of Cambridge, Massachusetts, receives no government support. It too is included in chapter 5 because it began as a hunger ministry. The Ministry Village of First Baptist Church in Leesburg, Florida, represents an all-inclusive ministry evangelism approach.

Ministry to the Homeless: An Interfaith Approach

If your congregation is small and your resources are limited, but you have a burden to help the homeless in your community, don't despair. Do what congregations in Whittier, California, do. Join with other congregations in your area to do what your church can't do alone.

Every winter since 1990, 15 to 20 member congregations of the Whittier Interfaith Council have united to sponsor the Interfaith Cold Weather Shelter to provide temporary housing for area homeless from October to March.

During the 1995–96 season, congregations involved included Episcopalian, Methodist, Baptist, Church of God, Latter Day Saints, Christian, Presbyterian, and Jewish. In past years, Roman Catholic and Lutheran congregations also have been involved. Most of the congregations are located within a two and one-half-mile radius of center city Whittier, a city of more than 70,000 people.

Because participating congregations differ in size and in available resources, each chooses its own level of involvement. Some congregations provide housing and meals for as many as four weeks a season; others provide housing and meals for one week only; others not equipped to provide housing chip in with food; and still others provide financial donations for the program.

It is an arrangement that has worked well for the congregations whose average Sunday morning attendances range from 125 to 500, according to Faith Conklin, current president of the Whittier Area Interfaith Council and pastor of Whittier United Methodist Church.

For example, Whittier Presbyterian, a congregation of 100 attendees with a median age of 60, takes a minimum of two weeks each winter. But, often when no other group is available, the congregation will take on as many as four weeks. When that happens, other congregations such as the Latter Day Saints provide the meals. Or, sometimes, Whittier Presbyterian will advertise in the local newspaper asking for help. Such an ad run in December 1995 brought forth an individual in the community who provided dinner for 50 homeless people three nights one week. "It's a touching story to see how the community responds," says Whittier Presbyterian's pastor, Jeff Nelson.

Greenleaf Avenue Baptist, a congregation with 125 to 150 people in Sunday worship, generally takes on only one week. What is remarkable is that as many as 75 volunteers pitch in to help. Since most of the church's members are retirees, that number is most of the physically able adults in the church.

Typically, each night 40 to 55 homeless people, including some families with children, find food and shelter through the interfaith ministry.

The schedule is the same for each week and at each location:

Doors open to the homeless each evening at 7:00 P.M. They leave the building each morning at 8:00 A.M.

Volunteers work in four shifts:

•Dinner, 7:00–8:00 P.M. (Cooks and their helpers arrive much earlier.)

•Bedding down, 8:00–9:00 P.M. At least 3 volunteers are needed to issue pallets and get everyone settled before lights out at 9:00.

•Night watch, 9:00 P.M.–7:00 A.M. At least 2 volunteers work this shift.

•Breakfast, 5:30. Volunteers arrive to prepare and serve breakfast and to make to-go lunches.

Over the years, those involved have learned:

•About interfaith cooperation.

Often, congregations like a Jewish synagogue or the Latter Day Saints that do not have adequate space to provide housing, prepare and serve the meals at the Presbyterian church, Nelson says. And for 4 years, a local Jewish-owned business provided food and staff for one week of the program as well. If an employee of the business volunteered to work the night shift, he or she could take the next day off from work with pay.

•About being realistic concerning the number of people the congregations can serve effectively.

After trying to serve as many as 75 in the early years, the program has settled in to serving 40 to 55 people. For a church of retirees such as Greenleaf Avenue Baptist, the short–term nature of the ministry is much more manageable than a long-term commitment.

•About screening the homeless.

At first, the rule was "everybody come," Nelson, of Whittier Presbyterian, says. But after continued problems with drinking, drugs and sex, the program now screens out those who will not comply with the rules. "We give them several chances to comply," he says. But if they don't, they cannot return. Problems have decreased dramatically.

•About maintaining good relationships with the community.

While there are always some problems to be ironed out between congregations and the surrounding community, a rotating shelter program reduces the perceived potential negative impact on the community.

•About effective use of facilities.

The first year Greenleaf Avenue Baptist participated in the program, the church used their fellowship hall for sleeping quarters. Now, a portion of the church building is blocked off for that purpose with separate rooms designated for families, husbands and wives, single men, and single women. This also eliminates the need to pick up and store sleeping pallets each day as well as giving the homeless a designated spot each night to call their own.

•About available resources.

"We have more resources than we thought," Nelson says. "Some senior citizens even have learned they can stay up all night."

Everyone in the church can get involved. Opportunities range from cooking to setting the tables to cleaning up to talking with the guests to taking the night watch.

Most of the food for the program comes from area food banks, and most of the congregations are able to pay additional costs such as utilities. Whittier Presbyterian also rents a portable toilet at $100 a week. The toilet is set up on the church parking lot for the homeless to use before the church doors open. The Interfaith Council received a one-time grant of $100,000 from the Federal Emergency Management Agency which was used to purchase 150 sleeping mats and to stockpile food staples. The money also is used to help some congregations with utilities, to pay to have the sleeping mats laundered regularly, and to pay college students to handle the screening process.

•About the long-term effect of the ministry.

Participating congregations have learned the problem of homelessness won't go away. They know they have not found the ultimate solution to the homeless situation in their community. In fact, some of the homeless people have been in the shelter program since its inception. "Sure it's a Band-aid approach," L. G. Chaddick, of Greenleaf Avenue Baptist, says. "But if a wound is open and bleeding, you need to have some primary care."

United Methodist pastor Conklin agrees. "This does not fix the problem. It's simply dealing with the up-front, visible need, not the root cause. But that doesn't mean we shouldn't be doing it." She would like to see a permanent shelter open in Whittier and also see the interfaith group get involved in shaping governmental policies.

•About staying true to the purpose of the program.

Chaddick well remembers the night he presented the idea of getting involved in the winter shelter program to Greenleaf Avenue Baptist's church lay leadership council. After he made his presentation, the council's chairperson made one simple statement: "I was hungry and you fed me." The group had no illusions that large numbers of the homeless would become Christians or that they would even come to their church. But, in spite of those realities, they knew they had to help.

•About how ingrained misconceptions about the homeless really are.

Such questions as Why don't they get jobs? reveal the "vast ignorance" on the subject of homelessness, Conklin says. "How quickly we forget what we are taught on Sunday and recite what we hear and the prevailing slogans of the culture."

•About perseverance and consistency.

One year, those virtues were put to the test at First United Methodist when members considered skipping out on housing during Christmas week. Finally, one woman said, "Yeah, let's just tell these people, in the name of Jesus, there's no place for them."

From then on, First United Methodist not only has provided housing on Christmas but has also kept their doors open all day and has provided a special Christmas dinner as well.

"I often tell my people, 'Ministry is inconvenient,'" Conklin says. "But, if Jesus were here, this is what He would be doing."

Ministry to the Homeless: One Man's Passion

Bill Woodward had seen one too many people sleeping in a car in his hometown of Williamsburg, Kentucky. He had to do something about it.

For 4 years, he had been seeking the missing piece of God's plan for his life after he had quit his job in a local factory to follow the call to preach. "I knew God had called me. I just didn't know where," Bill says.

The where came as he looked into the faces of the homeless people around him. And so, in 1990, Bill set up Emergency Christian Ministry (ECM) for the homeless in his town of 5,500 near the Tennessee border.

For almost a year, he worked through his local church helping the needy in the area. At the same time, he made plans to form a nonprofit organization to rent a house or mobile home to use in the ministry.

But Bill found "God had bigger and better plans." Rather than a rented house or mobile home, a motel would be home for ECM. And purchasing the motel would be the first of many steps of faith he would take in the ensuing years.

During the summer of 1991, he learned a 12-unit motel was on the market for $45,000 and that the Williamsburg City Council already had federal grant money in hand for a homeless program. So with $18 in the ECM bank account and a lot of faith, Bill approached the city council about securing the motel.

It took six months for him to convince the council that he could sustain a ministry to the homeless. "I had to prove we could do what we said we wanted to do," he says. But his faith and persistence paid off when the council offered to give $40,000 if Bill could get 10 local churches to support ECM with monthly donations for a year.

He did, and the ministry was off the ground and running. With two additional government grants totaling $90,000, ECM turned the motel into eight apartments, a kitchen, a dining room, and a clothing room.

Each month, ECM provides shelter for 60 to 80 people. Clients include single men, single women, single parents with children, and two-parent families with children. They stay for as few as one night to as many as 30 days. About half are locals who come from a 30- to 40-mile radius of

Williamsburg. House fires, evictions, family disputes, and spouse abuse all occasion the ministry of ECM.

The other half are travelers stranded on interstate 75, which runs near the town. "We've helped people from New York, California, and even Sweden," Bill says.

In addition, ECM helps as many as 200 people each month with emergency food and clothing. And each year during the Christmas holidays, the number of people helped swells. In November 1994, more than 500 people, nearly half of whom were children, turned to ECM. The ministry provided clothing for 365 people and food to 175, served 667 hot meals, and distributed 31 emergency food boxes. Every year, ECM works with local social service agencies to coordinate the town's Christmas food basket project.

Word gets out via the local police, clergy, and area newspapers. The ministry is a "tremendous referral point" for local churches, according to ECM board member Janus Jones. "The Lord seems to bring us the people who need us the most."

ECM operates on a shoestring staff and budget. A staff of four keeps ECM going: as director, Bill receives a part-time salary; a security guard receives a small stipend, room and board; both the cook and janitor are volunteers. Tenants help with chores. Laypersons and pastors from local churches serve on the interdenominational ministry's board of directors. Used clothing is donated by people in the community. And a dozen or so local churches each budget $20 to $150 a month which pulls the ministry through.

For Bill, the smiles on the faces of the people whose immediate needs have been met bring their own reward. But for the man who gave up his job to follow the call to preach, the icing on the cake is the 43 people who have made professions of faith in Christ over the last 4 years.

"One of our main desires is to lead people to the Lord," he said. "But you've got to meet physical needs before you can meet spiritual needs."

Ministry to the Poor: A Comprehensive Approach

Some churches say they care; First Baptist of Leesburg, Florida, shows they do. For more than 10 years, the church has been on a road of radical change from a traditional First Church to an innovative church which lives up to its motto: The Church That Cares. Today, more than 1,400 volunteers from the Leesburg congregation are involved in 82 different ministries. Ministries include the Rescue Mission, the Women's Care Center, the Children's Shelter and Teen Home, the Pregnancy-Care Center, and the Benevolence Ministry (a furniture barn, a clothing closet, and a food pantry). In mid-1995, the church completed the $2 million first phase of its new Ministry Village which will house some of the existing ministries which had been spread out in the more than 19 contiguous buildings the church had purchased over the past 15 years. And every single ministry's goal is not only to meet the needs of the people but to reach every person involved with the gospel of Jesus Christ.

For more than a decade, First Baptist's Christian Care Center, Inc., a nonprofit organization, has helped thousands of men, women, and children caught up in homelessness, hunger, poverty, abuse, abandonment, and crisis pregnancies. More than 1,000 children have come through the Children's Shelter; more than 1,000 women come to the Pregnancy Care Center each year; more than 300 men are served each year through the Rescue Mission; more than 100 women and children have been helped by the Women's Center over the past 10 years; and the benevolent ministries assist more than 5,000 a year.[14]

At first glance, one would think the church would have to be located in a major metropolitan center in order to need such a variety of ministries. But, that is not the case. Leesburg is small town USA, according to those who live there. Although the town is located about an hour from Orlando, it is not fast-growing, having experienced only a 6 percent growth rate over the past 10 years.[15] But the town has "a cross-section of every problem found in the United States," Pastor Charles Roesel says. " No area is immune anymore. We may be in the 'Bible Belt' but Satan is having a heyday. I've seen so many hurting people."[16]

The church models what it calls ministry evangelism.

"Ministry evangelism is not difficult to define, nor is it anything new," Charles Roesel wrote in the book, *Meeting Needs, Sharing Christ.* "Ministry evangelism is simply caring for persons in the name of Jesus Christ. It is meeting persons at the point of their need and ministering to them physically and spiritually. The intent of ministry evangelism is to present the good news of God's love in order to introduce persons to Jesus."[17]

It was a concept God "began laying on my heart over 15 years ago," Roesel says. Based in Matthew 25, it calls Christians to a life of sacrifice and service, not a life of ease. He calls it "the most effective way ever seen for reaching people for Jesus Christ."[18]

Ministry evangelism rests on two biblical foundations: the doctrines of the incarnation and the priesthood of the believer. "Ministry evangelism grows from our understanding of God as an incarnational, relating God and our understanding of ourselves, God's people, as God's ministers who are called to bring others to the Father's love," Roesel wrote.[19]

"It is not a kind of social gospel or rice-bowl Christianity," Roesel says. "We are there to love persons and to minister to them. Even if they do not make a decision for Christ, we are still going to minister to them. We want to do more than just minister to the physical needs they have. We want them to know Jesus. The only way they can have eternal peace and joy is through Him. We see no conflict at all in meeting human needs and the real need of their soul."[20]

Moving from a traditional First Church mentality to the present ministry evangelism mentality did not happen without struggle. At first "half the church was for it and half against it," according to minister of evangelism Art Ayris. Some church members resisted the idea of reaching hurting people. Art remembers some saying, "These aren't our kind of people," and others saying, "I don't like to have my wife walk by these kind of people to get into the church." Too, in those days, the church was not large; it averaged only about 300 people in Sunday School.

And so, Roesel prayed and preached and waited for God to change the hearts of his people. "You don't start such a change with a divided church," Art says.

And change they did. Now Pastor Roesel says he's "afraid to mention a ministry unless I mean business because I'm guaranteed the people will do it." He cites the time he tested the waters on ministry to people with AIDS and the deacons said, "If this comes up in our community, let's go for it."[21]

Another Homeless Ministry Model

A Living Christmas Tree. Each Christmas, Southside Baptist Church in Jacksonville, Florida, plans a special presentation of their Living Christmas Tree for the homeless of their city.

The church contacts the city's rescue missions and homeless shelters and arranges to pick up the homeless. At the church, they serve their guests a nice, sit-down meal before presenting "The Living Christmas Tree." Between 300 and 500 people attend, "depending on how cold the weather is," according to minister Eddie Lockamy.

Afterwards, each guest is given a gift of hygiene items and a New Testament.

In March 1995, the church received a letter from a homeless woman who had attended the event the previous year. She said that in the three months since the presentation, she had found a job and an apartment and had got her life together. She wrote to thank the church and enclosed one dollar to "put toward this year's presentation."

Put Your Faith to Work

If you want to minister to the homeless, . . .
Pray

•For yourself. Ask God to reveal your blindspots about homeless people. Was there a time in your life when you were more open to helping the homeless? Have you succumbed to compassion fatigue? Are you too comfortable to care? Ask God to show you what specific contribution He wants you to make to minister to the homeless.

•For ministries with the homeless. Ask God to give strength and wisdom to those who are giving their lives to bring light and life to the homeless.

•For governmental leaders who deal with homelessness.

Become an advocate for the homeless (see p. 21 for how to be an effective advocate).

Proverbs 31:8–9 (NIV) says, "Speak up for those who cannot speak for themselves, for the rights of all who are destitute. Speak up and judge fairly; defend the rights of the poor and needy."

•Get the facts about homelessness. Don't let the complexity of the issue deter you from seeking God-given ways to get involved.

•Write your local, state, and national legislators with your specific concerns and suggestions. "Defend the poor and fatherless: do justice to the afflicted and needy. Deliver the poor and needy: rid them out of the hand of the wicked" (Psalm 82:3–4).

Get involved in hands-on ministry.

•Conduct a needs awareness survey/tour of your community to discover what the homeless situation really is. Get involved in an existing ministry or begin a ministry to address unmet needs.

•Contact your local, regional, or national denominational headquarters. Find out what is being done for the homeless and how you can plug in.

Use the list below as a springboard for hands-on ministry. Some of the ministries suggested require the aid of professionals such as medical personnel or social work professionals. Some will require state and local governmental approval. Some involve more liability than others so make certain your church insurance provides coverage for these ministries. (These ideas require minimal time involvement and may serve as entry points for ministry to the homeless or as onetime ministries.)

HEALTH AND HYGIENE MINISTRIES

•Mammogram screening. Provide a mobile mammogram unit.

•Dental care. Set up a free dental clinic or provide a mobile clinic.

•Vision care. Set up a free eye care clinic or provide a mobile clinic. Work with local vision centers to secure free eyeglasses.

•Health screening. Set up free screenings for blood pressure and cholesterol for the homeless.

•Personal care kits. Assemble kits with such items as toothpaste, toothbrush, soap, and shaving supplies to distribute at homeless shelters.

•Showers and laundry. Outfit your church with showers and washers and dryers for the homeless to use. Provide soap, towels, and laundry detergent.

•Haircuts. Provide free haircuts.

•Clothes. Set up an attractive clothing center.

FOOD

•Soup kitchen. Open your church kitchen as a soup kitchen one night a week. Use your church bus or van to transport the homeless as guests to the meal.

•Bag lunches. Prepare bag lunches and distribute them to the homeless in your community. The weekend is a good time to distribute these since most free food programs do not operate on the weekend.

•Restaurant vouchers. Work with local restaurants to provide vouchers for meals for the homeless.

•Holiday meals. Provide holiday meals for the homeless at the church or in your home.

•Free food. Become a "gleaner." Work with local grocery stores, restaurants, hotels, and catering companies to secure unsold bread and perishables to give away.

SUPPORT

•Support groups. Open your church building to groups such as Alcoholics Anonymous, literacy training, and vocational rehabilitation.

•Reading rooms. Open a reading room in your church building for the homeless.

EMPLOYMENT SERVICES

•Mailboxes, telephone. Provide mailboxes and a telephone number which jobless persons can use for job referrals.

TEMPORARY HOUSING

•Open your church facilities to the homeless on cold nights.

PERMANENT HOUSING

•HUD housing. Your church can become a homeless provider through the US Department of Housing and Urban Development (HUD). A HUD house can be leased for $1 a year. The church pays property taxes and utilities while subleasing the home to a homeless family. Contact the HUD office in your area for details.

Selected Resources on Ministry to the Homeless

The following resources offer specific, detailed help on how to get started in ministry with the homeless.

Books

Atkinson, Donald A., and Charles L. Roesel. *Meeting Needs, Sharing Christ.* Nashville: LifeWay Press, 1995. A comprehensive treatment of the theology as well as the practical aspects of the ministry of First Baptist Church in Leesburg, Florida.

Bock, Betty. *You Can Make a Difference.* Birmingham, AL: Woman's Missionary Union, 1992.

Temple, Gray, Jr. *Fifty-two Ways to Help Homeless People.* Nashville: Thomas Nelson, 1991.

Pamphlets

Pittman, Tobey. "How Your Church Can Minister with Homeless People." Alpharetta, GA: Home Mission Board.

"Beginning a Ministry with Homeless People." Alpharetta, GA: Home Mission Board.

Journal Articles

Bailey, Patricia L. "Social Work Practice in Community Ministries." As cited in Garland, Diana R. *Church Social Work.* St. Davids. PA: North American Association of Christians in Social Work, 1992. Addresses issues which need to be considered in developing interdenominational community ministries.

Principles of Service to the Homeless

•It nearly always takes longer than you planned. There are no quick fixes. Be prepared to spend much time and labor if you want to make a lasting difference.
•It generally will cost more than was anticipated. And the cost will not only be financial, but also giving yourself.

•It is generally messier than you anticipate. You cannot separate homeless persons from their problems. You must work with both. Beneath the obvious need for shelter are problems which may range from drug addiction to crime to divorce to joblessness.

•It requires a greater determination than you expected. When the glamour wears off, "pure determination and dedication to complete the task have to take over."

Source: Carl R. Resener, *Crisis in the Streets* (Nashville: Broadman Press, 1988), 139–41.

The Bible and the Poor

The Bible says:

•SHARE the burden of the poor by sharing one's resources with the poor (Job 31:15; Matt. 5:42; 19:21).

•CARE about the outcome of the poor and needy (Luke 16:20; Zech. 7:10; Lev. 25:25; Acts 20:35; John 12:6; Lev. 19:9; Deut. 15:11; Rom. 12:20).

•BEAR some of the burdens of the poor and needy (Psalm 112:4; Prov. 31:9; Isa. 1:17; 16:3; Luke 14:12; James 2:2–16; 5:4).

Source: Carl R. Resener, *Crisis in the Streets* (Nashville: Broadman Press, 1988), 158.

On any given day, who are the homeless?

- 66 to 75 percent single men
- 15 to 20 percent families with children, 80 percent of whom are single women with children
- Less than 10 percent single women
- 4 percent unaccompanied youth (usually boys 12 to 18 years old)

- 51 percent black
- 35 percent white
- 14 percent other

- Twenty-four (24) percent are employed in full- or part-time jobs.
- Twenty-five (25) percent are veterans.
- Fifty (50) percent have not finished high school.
- Twenty (20) percent of single homeless have been hospitalized for mental problems.
- Thirty-five (35) percent have been treated for chemical dependency.
- Fifty-five (55) percent have been in jail five or more days.
- Twenty-five (25) percent have served time in state or federal prisons.
- Seventy-five (75) percent of the adults with children are nonwhite and predominantly female.
- Thirty (30) to 40 percent suffer from serious mental illness such as schizophrenia, manic depression, or clinical depression.

Sources: 1987 Urban Institute study; 1993 US Department of Veterans Affairs study.

Homelessness: A Chronology

1930s

The federal government begins to provide a wide range of programs for transients and the homeless:

•1933—There are 1.2 million homeless people in mid-January.

•1933–35—The Federal Emergency Relief Administration (FERA) provides shelter, food, medical care, clothing, cash, and jobs for 375,000 people.

•1935—FERA is replaced with specialized programs such as Works Progress Administration and the Social Security Act, establishing for the first time an ongoing relief role for the federal government.

1960s

Pensions, unemployment insurance, Medicaid, and Medicare help decrease the number of homeless. But the passage of the Community Health Centers Act deinstitutionalizes an estimated 430,000 mentally ill people, and many of them end up on the streets.

1970s

The courts become involved in homelessness for the first time in the history of the US:

•1972—The US Supreme Court decriminalized vagrancy and ruled that laws requiring residency as a condition for receiving assistance are unconstitutional.

•1979—The first right-to-shelter lawsuit was filed in New York State Supreme Court which resulted in a December 5 ruling that the state and city must provide "clean bedding, wholesome food, and adequate supervision and security." Within ten days, New York City opened its first public shelter in 50 years on Ward's Island.

1980s

The nation awakens to the plight of the homeless:

•1981—A study of New York City's homeless population garners national attention.

•September 1982—A controversial survey by the Community for Creative Non-Violence in Washington, D.C., contends that 1 percent of the population is homeless.

•October 1982—A 55-city survey by the US Conference of Mayors reveals that only 43 percent of the demand for emergency services for the homeless is being met.

•May 1984—The Department of Housing and Urban Development estimates the homeless to number 250,000 to 350,000.

•July 1987—Congress passes the Stewart B. McKinney Homeless Assistance Act. The Act is reauthorized for an additional two years in November 1988.

1990s

The shift continues from an emergency response to looking for long-term solutions:

•1990—Congress reauthorizes the McKinney Act.

•May 1992—The US Census Bureau releases the results of a nationwide survey of homeless people taken the night of March 20, 1990. The snapshot of the homeless showed 459,000 in shelters and on the street.

Source: *Congressional Quarterly Researcher,* August 7, 1992, 673.

Notes

[1] *Congressional Quarterly Researcher,* August 7, 1992, 669.
[2] Ibid., 671.
[3] Frank and Janet Ferrell, *Trevor's Place: The Story of the Boy Who Brings Hope to the Homeless* (San Francisco: Harper and Row Publishers, 1985).
[4] *Congressional Quarterly Researcher,* August 7, 1992, 673.
[5] Ibid., 669.
[6] Ibid., 670–71.
[7] "Homelessness Facts Quiz," prepared by Eric N. Lindblom, homelessness policy analyst at the US Department of Veterans Affairs, Washington, DC, 1993.
[8] Carl R. Resener, *Crisis in the Streets* (Nashville: Broadman Press, 1988), 31–42.

[9] *Congressional Quarterly Researcher,* August 7, 1992, 672–73.

[10] Ibid., 672.

[11] Ibid., 676.

[12] "Can Charity Fill the Gap?" *Time,* December 4, 1995, 44–45.

[13] Ibid.

[14] Michael Chute, "A Church with Heart," *Florida Baptist Witness,* October 5, 1995, 4.

[15] Donald A. Atkinson and Charles L. Roesel, *Meeting Needs, Sharing Christ* (Nashville: LifeWay Press, 1995), 9.

[16] Chute, "A Church with Heart," 5.

[17] Atkinson and Roesel, *Meeting Needs,* 10.

[18] Chute, "A Church with Heart," 5.

[19] Atkinson and Roesel, *Meeting Needs,* 11.

[20] Ibid., 26.

[21] Chute, "A Church with Heart," 5.

Dear Norma (not her real name):

I doubt you will remember me, but I certainly remember you.

Nine years ago, I went to a crisis center for problem pregnancies. I wasn't married and was four months pregnant; my family was furious and pushing to give the baby up for adoption. I desperately needed some love and support, and *you were there!*

There are no words to describe what you did for me. Your love and support and prayers gave me the strength I needed. Today, I have a beautiful eight-year-old boy. He and his sister are the light of my life. I am crying as I write this letter. I can't imagine not having my son with me. You held my hand and were there for me during a difficult time in my life, when I lost my family because I chose to keep my child. (You were right—my family did eventually come around.)

Thank you doesn't seem sufficient for what you did for me. God has blessed me with two wonderful children, a career, and a very full life. I can only hope you, too, have been blessed with great happiness.

I have enclosed a photo of the baby you saved and my daughter, the baby who carries your name.

Thank you and God bless you.

Jill (not her real name)

"The girls who come through the doors of a crisis pregnancy center think they are coming for the free pregnancy test, but they really are coming for someone to listen to them."

—Lou Allard, director of the Crisis Pregnancy Center in Oklahoma City

3

*V*aluing Life

She could be your sister, daughter, niece, cousin, neighbor, friend, church member, or perhaps even you. She could be any age past puberty and before menopause, a member of any race or religion, any educational level or social background."[1]

She thinks she's pregnant. Her boyfriend, parents, and peers are sure they know what she should do. They tell her to get an abortion.

She is not alone. Since the 1973 *Roe v. Wade* Supreme Court decision legalizing abortion, millions of girls and women have faced that moment—and opted to abort their babies. Every year, more than 1 million women in the United States deny their unborn babies the right to life. Nationwide, the current rate of abortions is estimated at 25.9 per 1,000 women aged 15 to 44.[2]

And while a 1995 report from the nonprofit Alan Guttmacher Institute said that both the number of abortions and abortion providers has declined since 1992, there are still at least 2,300 abortion providers in the United States, according to their count. The institute, which is affiliated with Planned Parenthood, said the 1992 total number of abortions was a decrease of 28,000, or 1.8 percent, from the previous year. The number of abortion providers was said to have dropped 18 percent from 1982 to 1992, from 2,908 to 2,380.[3]

In the years since 1973, abortion has stepped to center stage, becoming a high-profile political and moral issue which has polarized the nation. According to a 1993 Gallup Poll, the majority (51 percent) of Americans take a middle ground—that abortion is justified in some circumstances. Among the remainder of the population, 32 percent believe abortion should be legal in all circumstances.[4]

The abortion issue has polarized Christians. Even conservative Christians do not agree. According to the same Gallup Poll, even the self-proclaimed "intensely religious" are divided, with 55 percent believing abortion should be legal under certain circumstances; 22 percent believe abortion should be legal under any circumstances; and 19 percent believing it should be illegal in all circumstances.[5]

But for each Jane or Sue or Norma who faces that moment of truth, abortion is no longer a political football. The questions are no longer philosophical or theoretical, or even theological. The crisis is personal; the questions real. Who can I turn to? Where can I go for help? Who will listen?

In many communities the Janes and Sues and Normas have somewhere other than an abortion clinic to turn for help because of the concern of Christians ministering through crisis pregnancy centers and homes for unwed mothers. The past decade has seen a significant multiplication of efforts to offer alternatives to women making choices surrounding unplanned pregnancies.

In the process of getting involved in crisis pregnancy and alternatives to abortion ministries, concerned Christians have learned there are no easy answers when a woman faces an unplanned pregnancy.

In her book *No Easy Choices,* Sylvia Boothe says: "There are no easy answers once there is an [unplanned] pregnancy. All of the options carry difficulties. There are no pat answers."[6]

There are options, however. Sylvia, who is coordinator of the Alternatives to Abortion Ministries with the Home Mission Board of the Southern Baptist Convention, lists three alternatives to abortion options, along with potential difficulties:

•Single parenting

Single parenting can bring many rewards, but raising a child alone is hard work and demands many sacrifices.

•Marriage

Most teenage marriages end in divorce. An early marriage between a couple may be the answer, but not for every couple.

•Adoption

Adoption can be a loving choice, but it can be a painful choice for the birth mother.[7]

While abortion clinics have captured the attention of the media, Kay Coles James claims in her book *Transforming America from the Inside Out* that "for every abortion clinic that exists in America today there is a crisis-pregnancy center that is designed to help those same women and those same children."[8]

Centers generally fall into two categories: extension, or alternate-location, crisis pregnancy centers and independent centers. An extension center operates under the auspices of a local church or group of churches. An independent crisis pregnancy center is a ministry operating under a local board of directors. An extension center may or may not be incorporated separately from its parent organization. An independent center is independently incorporated and functions under the authority of a board of directors whose members represent several area churches.[9] Most centers of both types are located in neutral settings, away from church buildings or abortion clinics. Many choose high visibility and easily accessible locations. Advertising is done primarily through telephone yellow pages, although some centers utilize highway billboards. Common names for centers include *Crisis Pregnancy Center, Pregnancy Help Center,* and *Pregnancy Testing Center.* Other names, though not an exhaustive listing, include *Hope Center, Life Centers,* and *New Beginnings.*

Center staff usually includes a paid director and a minimum of 25 volunteer trained counselors. Hours of operation range from 20 hours to 60 hours per week, depending on need and volunteers available to work.

Models in this chapter include extension centers under the auspices of First Baptist Church in Orlando, Florida; First Baptist Church of Euliss, Texas; and the Baptist General Convention of Oklahoma. The Pregnancy Aid South Suburbs Assist Services in Tinley Park (Chicago), Illinois, represents the many independent nonprofit centers across the country.

The United States has one of the highest rates of unintended childbearing of any nation in the industrialized world. "The proportion of pregnancies that are unwanted or mistimed ranges from 40 percent among married women to 88 percent among never-married women," according to the *New York Times*. The *Times* also reports that illegitimate births have increased from 18 percent of births in 1980 to 31 percent today. While the vast majority of women having children outside marriage are poor or working class and poorly educated, they are also diverse. Nearly 40 percent are non-Hispanic white and 54 percent are in their 20s.[10]

Teenagers account for about one-third of all unmarried mothers, Black teenagers about 12 percent. Out-of-wedlock childbearing is rising fastest among women 20 and older, who now account for seven of every ten out-of-wedlock births, according to the February 11, 1996, *Times* report.[11]

Arguments now are raging over whether such numbers indicate a breakdown in morality in the United States or whether they are a function of economics which causes "young adults [to] increasingly view marriage as an ideal that is beyond their grasp," as the *Times* article suggests.[12]

For some Christians, these numbers do represent a moral breakdown which must be addressed. Shiphrah Ministries in Belton, South Carolina, is included in this chapter as an inspiring model of one woman's God-given dream come true to provide a home and an opportunity for a new beginning for pregnant teens.

To Be Wanted and Loved

"You took two lives." The thought ran through Harriet Dial like the pain of a fist strategically placed between her shoulder blades as she continued her Sunday morning run.

For Harriet, that realization was a Jacoblike encounter with God that would change her life.

"Harriet, what is the worst thing you can do?" she heard God saying to her.

"Lord, there are no 'worst things.' Sin is sin."

"Then, what is the best?"

"Greater love hath no man than this, that a man lay down his life for a friend" (John 15:13 KJV).

"Then, what's the worst?"

"To take a life. And I have taken two. I have had two abortions."

Later than morning, Harriet went to church, unaware that it was Sanctity of Life Sunday. There, her earlier impressions were confirmed. "I had never before made the connection between abortion and murder," she said.

Although she had joined a church at age 10, Harriet had never really made a commitment to Christ. By the time she was 29, she had been on drugs, had two abortions, and become a single mom. Life had taken her from her native Georgia to Alaska to Texas.

In Texas, some church women took an interest in her and helped her turn her life to God. They took her to lunch, listened to her arguments about the Bible and God, and "mothered me up into the Lord," she says. Through those women, Harriet became a believer. Because of them, she moved from a career in physical education to an interest in a counseling career.

At about the same time, her daughter chose to go to a college in North Carolina. So together they moved, thinking Harriet could find a job, as well as work on a counseling degree.

But that was not to be. No job materialized, and over the next 3 years, Harriet lost everything she owned. Finally, a job opened at an alcoholic rehabilitation center for teens. During the 5 years she worked there, God began to lay a ministry to pregnant teens on her heart. "He said, 'Step out and do it,' but I ran from it," she says.

Instead, Harriet opened a shelter for battered women. Although the shelter was successful, Harriet believes her involvement "wasn't of the Lord." She was meeting needs, but still she was running from God. "The whole time," she says, "the Lord was telling me my work was with teens."

The entire time, she knew why she was running from God: she carried a secret she knew she would need to reveal if she opened a home for unwed teens. It was a secret she wanted to keep, because "by then, people in North Carolina thought I was a pretty good person," she says. It was a secret she thought she had left behind when she moved back East.

Then came that Sunday morning run and that defining conversation with her God. As never before, Harriet knew what God wanted her to do. But still, she procrastinated.

Another year passed before Harriet said yes to God. At a performance of Handel's *Messiah,* she once again heard the voice of God asking her how she could know all she did and not "go tell."

That night, Harriet went home for a final struggle with God as she contemplated what would become of her if she followed His leading. Would she be destitute if she started the ministry? She walked from room to room, pausing to consider the importance of each item she had accumulated. "Will I still be Harriet if I don't have this sofa?" she mused. She says she faced her toughest battle with self when she reached her clothes closet. "Will I have to wear the same shoes for the next 40 years?"

Then she prayed and put out a Gideonlike fleece to God: she asked Him to give her a name for the ministry. If He did, she said she would procrastinate no longer. She was led to read about the birth of Moses in Exodus 1; there, she found the name Shiphrah. Shiphrah: an Israelite midwife; a midwife whom God raised up over 4,000 years ago to save babies; a name which means "beauty."

For Harriet, the long struggle was over. It had taken at least 5 years for her to work through the guilt and shame of her decisions to abort two babies. Often, she "had no idea how to move on," but clung to the Scriptures believing that "God would tell me what to do." Healing came, she says, as she "stayed in the Word, struggling with the fact that abortion is wrong but there is healing in Jesus Christ."

Finally, at age 40, Harriet was able to leave the past behind and move forward. "There was power in the 'laying down'" of the past, she says, as she left behind her baggage and trusted God. She knew, too, that God wanted to use the story of her past as a means of bringing healing in the lives of other women.

She quit her job and enrolled in Erskine Theological Seminary in Due West, South Carolina. By this time, her daughter had completed her doctorate, and Harriet felt God had released her from those financial responsibilities.

A friend provided a place for her to live and money to live on. That first year in seminary, Harriet used every available free moment to lay the groundwork for her future ministry. She visited maternity homes to glean the best ideas. She researched licensing policies, medical and facility needs. She studied how best to teach the girls about Jesus.

During that first year she met a benefactor whom God would use to give her the start she needed—and in the process teach her that God always would know better than she what she would need. Dick Smith, a Baptist layman and car dealer from Columbia, South Carolina, and his wife Wilma Smith offered 52 acres in Belton, South Carolina.

Land wasn't exactly want Harriet had hoped for. "I thought I needed a house, but God gave me land," she says. It was a gift which would shape the direction of Shiphrah Ministries in ways only God could know.

Shiphrah Ministries began officially in 1988. The first residential home for unwed mothers opened in the homeplace of a member of First Baptist Church in Belton in September 1989. Harriet had prayed that God would send seven girls for that first home; instead, He sent two. The ministry moved to the 52 acres when the first permanent home was built.

That was God's second lesson. "I was despondent, but God soon showed me I had just enough faith for two, and I would grow in my faith."

Those lessons were the first of many Harriet would learn in how to trust God—lessons about:

The need for the ministry and the girls who could benefit most from Shiphrah Ministries.

The home is the only licensed Christian home in South Carolina to take in pregnant girls under 18 years of age. Many of the girls are hard cases which most other Christian homes will not take. Girls learn about the home through billboard advertisements, referrals from James Dobson's Focus on the Family, and word of mouth. The home initially was licensed to care for 14 girls who could stay from 9 months to 1 year. With the opening of a new unit in February 1996, Shiphrah now can care for 8 more girls.

The shape the ministry should take.

The farm environment has afforded the opportunity for Shiphrah Ministries not only to be a home in which the unwed mothers can live until their babies are born but also a classroom in which to learn how to break the cycle of poverty in which many of them are caught.

One girl said it well, "It was the first time in my life I'd ever seen anything to the finish. I learned to live, interact, relate, forgive, understand, and love. I came to know Jesus."

While the girls don't have to pay for their expenses, each is required to work while at Shiphrah. In order to underscore the desire to teach the girls how to get off welfare, the ministry doesn't accept any government money.

Work opportunities include:

•A licensed dairy with a show-quality herd of Nubian and Alpine goats. The girls milk the goats. Future plans call for the dairy to expand to include cheese processing. The products would be consumed by the residents as well as sold in the ministry's gift shop.

•A vegetable garden. The girls grow much of the food they consume. In 1995, in addition to the food they grew and ate during the summer months, they processed more than 300 jars of food to use during the winter. They also sold their products at a produce stand.

•A craft shop. Girls make crafts which they sell in the shop called "All God's Creatures."

•"All God's Children." Girls wash and iron infant wear to give, along with a Bible, to needy families in the community.

Harriet's goal is for the ministry to be 50 percent self-supporting with the remaining money coming from donations.

The scope of the ministry.

While the ministry began as a home for pregnant teens, it has expanded to include a fully licensed school for the girls. The school too has grown beyond Harriet's wildest dreams.

What she envisioned as little more than a homebound school meeting around her dining room table has developed into portable classrooms where the girls can complete their GEDs. Each girl is required to attend the on-campus school. One full-time teacher guides them through the PACE program. The school has a computer program, a library, and a home economics department. In 1994, 13 girls completed high school and went on to college. Shiphrah helped them with paperwork for scholarships, grants, or student loans. The ministry often helps pay book fees and supplies clothes.

The financial base for the ministry.

Shiphrah Ministries is a faith-ministry operation with a board of directors. Fund-raising is done "on our knees," Harriet says. But she acknowledges that learning to trust God is a continual lesson.

She often tells how she "fussed with God" when she didn't have money in hand to pay for moving the first portable classroom to the farm.

One morning when she was on her usual 5:00 A.M. trip to the barn to milk the goats, she told God she still was short most of the money needed to move the classroom. "The Lord told me I didn't need the money that day since the building hadn't been delivered yet."

The next Sunday morning, a couple whose daughter had lived at Shiphrah gave Harriet an envelope. When she got around to opening it about 9:00 that night, she found $1,000—exactly what she needed to pay to move the classroom.

The money had come from the interest on a trust fund which the girl's grandfather had set up for her education. Now, the interest on that money was placed in Harriet's hands to provide a place for other girls to complete high school.

Emotional, physical, and spiritual strength for the ministry. Shiphrah has been Harriet's life.

It is a 24-hour-a-day, seven-day-a-week ministry. For years, Harriet has taken only one day off each year— Christmas Day. But now, with five full-time and part-time assistants, she hopes soon to take one day a week off.

She admits it is hard work which she could never do without God's help. Some mornings when the alarm goes off at 4:00 A.M., she's too tired to get up . . . she thinks. But then she sees the crucifix hanging above her bed, and strength comes for yet another day. "If my Lord could hang there for me for six hours, then surely I can get my feet on the floor."

The will to keep on dreaming.

More than 200 girls and women aged 10 to 24 have been ministered to in the name of Jesus in the more than 5 years Shiphrah has been in operation. More than 4,000 girls have been assisted with housing, food, clothing, baby needs, and education.

But that is just a drop in the bucket for what Harriet hopes the ministry will accomplish long term. Over the next 10 years, she would like to open ten more homes in other locations. She wants the first of those to be for babies with AIDS. And she would like each of the homes to focus on high-risk juvenile offenders, the girls few people seem to want to help.

"If you come to visit Shiphrah, you will walk through well-maintained pastures and barns, down the graveled path into the sparkling hallway of the main building, and you will be struck with awe at the many things being accomplished, against all odds, in this place," one visitor wrote. But more than that, she wrote, you will be reminded that "It is a remarkable ministry—because we have a remarkable God."

A remarkable God—that too is what Harriet Dial would want you to remember.

For More Than a Test

"The girls who come through the doors of a crisis pregnancy center think they are coming for the free pregnancy test, but they really are coming for someone to listen to them," says Lou Allard, director of the Crisis Pregnancy Center in Oklahoma City which has been open since April 1986. The center is 1 of more than 100 operated by Southern Baptist groups across the country.

It takes a while for most to open up and tell a stranger their innermost fears. Often, a scheduled 30-minute session stretches into 2, 3, or 4 hours. Once, for example, a 15-year-old started out saying her dog had bitten her. And before she got around to saying she was afraid she was pregnant, the girl had told many things that were happening in her life. "She was saying she was hurting and needed help," Lou said. "She was asking me if I would accept her for who she was that day."

While a free pregnancy test is what gets most girls and women through the door, it is only one of the ministry services provided at crisis pregnancy centers. Center personnel offer information, education, and counseling that ensures confidentiality and describes all options open to the mother. They give practical assistance such as referrals to lawyers and adoption agencies and necessities such as infant care items, food, and clothing. They offer spiritual guidance when the client is receptive. They provide complete information on the implications of carrying the baby to term or of having an abortion, including medical facts on abortion, abortion procedures, and potential consequences. And, in some centers, they provide sex education programs.

Extension Crisis Pregnancy Centers

In Orlando, Florida

In Orlando, First Baptist's Center for Pregnancy sees more than 2,000 clients per year. The three paid staff persons are considered a part of the First Baptist staff and are paid by the church. The center's 1996 budget of $30,000 is a line item in First Baptist's budget. In addition, the church pays staff salaries and the phone bill, and charges no rent for the facilities. Thirty-five volunteers work with the staff persons to make possible these services:

•First Steps. Postabortion support group program written by the center's first director, Lynn Kennedy. Currently, two groups meet each week. Center director Sandy Epperson leads one; Mertzie Levell, a Roman Catholic, leads the other.

•HOPE. An accountability program. "This breathed new life into our ministry," Sandy says. "HOPE makes the girls accountable and us better stewards." In order to receive things such as diapers, infant formula, clothing, and baby beds, center clients may earn coupons by:

•Monthly support meetings. Community professionals speak on subjects ranging from finances to single parenting to pregnancy issues. Fifteen to 20 women attend the 1½-hour meeting.

•Weekly Bible study. This has evolved into a support group for pregnant and postpregnant women. Eight to 10 women attend regularly.

•Viewing videotapes on child rearing, exercise, etc. The 15-minute tapes are available from the center library during the hours the center is open.

•Legal and adoption referrals. While the center is not an adoption agency, personnel do make referrals to lawyers and adoption agencies as a part of giving clients alternatives to abortion.

Volunteers from First Baptist provide a Sunday School-type experience for children during the monthly meeting and weekly Bible study.

Counselors are trained to share the gospel with any client who grants permission to do so. "We are very tender about the fact that the women come to us for specific help," Sandy says, "Yet, we want them to see the hope that is in Christ." If a client refuses to hear the gospel, "we understand and help anyway," she says.

In more than 5 years as center director, Sandy says her best advice to anyone wishing to minister in a crisis pregnancy center is to "Keep your eyes on the Lord." Don't be blown away by the heavy circumstances of clients' lives. "You can't solve all their problems, but He will," she said.

In Euliss, Texas

In Euliss, Texas, since First Baptist's Crisis Pregnancy Center opened in August 1984, counselors have seen more than 20,000 clients (2,400 to 3,000 a year or 200 to 250 per month). Unlike the Orlando center, the Euliss center is not in the church budget, but is included as a designated item on offering envelopes used by church members. Half the center's income comes from church members and the paid staff are considered part of the church staff, according to center director Paula Odom. "I like being under the umbrella of the church," she says. "They help with decisions and are there for me."

Prayer is the backbone of the ministry, Paula says. Many First Baptist members volunteer as prayer warriors. Some participate in a prayer chain which is activated when a need arises; others use the prayer room at First Baptist; others pray for the ministry as they go about the chores of their daily lives.

"Do not take a life" is the word the ministry stands on. "We can trust that word," Paula says. "It is solid." While she says center personnel "point people to the truth in love," they are careful not to "shine a light in people's faces," lest they can't see the way.

"We want to shine the light so they can see the path to God," she says.

Trust in the sovereignty of God is the advice Paula gives her volunteer counselors. "If we share the truth and a girl still aborts, we've been faithful to our call," she says. "We don't have to carry the burden of her decision on our shoulders. Only God can change the heart. He can still reach that girl."

As in all the crisis pregnancy ministries modeled in this chapter, volunteers make the ministry possible. Fifty volunteer counselors work in the center. They are involved with a client from the first moment she walks through the door of the center. If a client chooses to give birth, volunteers keep in touch via notes and phone calls throughout the pregnancy. If the client keeps her baby, volunteers are available to help her learn to care for the infant and for herself as a new mother.

In addition to free pregnancy testing, some of the services offered are:
- Single parenting classes
- Extensive adoption referrals
- A clothing room with baby and maternity clothes
- Sexual abstinence education for church youth groups
- Postabortion counseling
- Bible study groups

In Oklahoma City

He told her to spend the weekend in prayer and then go to minister either at a jail or at a women's shelter at 9:00 on Monday morning. "I knew I didn't want to go to a jail, so I went to a women's shelter," Lou Allard says. But she wanted to be a missionary, and she had made her feelings public at a worship service. That decision prompted the counselor's unusual instructions to her.

That Monday morning, Lou found her ministry. She became a volunteer counselor at the Crisis Pregnancy Center in Oklahoma City operated by the Baptist General Convention of Oklahoma. Four years later, in 1992, she became the center's director.

The center offers many of the same services as the Florida and Texas centers modeled in this chapter. As in those two centers, volunteers are key. Lou takes volunteers "where they are with their particular gifts" and trains them to do what is needed. One requirement, however, is non-negotiable. Volunteers must agree to maintain contact with clients who choose to have their babies until the babies are born if the clients give permission. Lou feels so strongly that this contact is essential to the well-being of the clients that she tells potential volunteers if they cannot commit to staying in touch with clients, then "we can't use you."

Staying in touch often means a volunteer goes to the hospital when a client has her baby. Volunteers are invited to many clients' baby showers. And center volunteers receive more than a few wedding invitations.

Other services offered by the center include:
•Job referral.
•Shepherding homes for girls who need a temporary place to live.
•Educational opportunities in conjunction with area vocational/technical schools.
•Baby furniture.
•Referrals for ongoing counseling.
•Assistance in obtaining medical services.
•Sexual abstinence education in the public schools and at youth retreats at the Baptist General Convention of Oklahoma's retreat facilities.

When Lou is invited to a school, she makes keynote presentations and spends up to 6 hours in classrooms. For senior high school students, she offers AIDS and sexual abstinence information; for middle school students, she teaches how to say no to pressure to have sex. As a part of her preparation, she attends parent-teacher meetings and school board meetings to learn what parents want. She encourages parents to attend the sessions she leads in the schools and to evaluate the program.

The problem, she says, is not teen pregnancy; it's teen sex. Her message is simple: God's plan is one man, one woman, one life. During the 1994–95 school year, Lou spoke in 56 public schools. Although she cannot mention the name of God in her presentations, she finds plenty of opportunity to do so in one-on-one conversations with students afterwards. "Then I am able to minister in Jesus' name," she says.

Lou has found the same message is needed at church-run camps. "If you think 'good kids' aren't involved in sex, you're wrong," she says. She cites her experiences when she spoke 38 times in three weeks one summer at Falls Creek Assembly, an Oklahoma Baptist camp. During one week, she gave three pregnancy tests, counseled 7 women who had aborted babies, talked with 6 men who were working at the camp who had paid for abortions for their girlfriends, and counseled 2 women who currently were involved in affairs with their pastors. Both women had had abortions.

"It's so sad that we don't want to realize we have hurting people in our churches," she says.

That hurt, Lou knows firsthand. Often, clients will sense an "identifying spirit." They ask her how she could know so well what they are feeling. Her knowledge is born of personal pain—as a child, she was molested repeatedly by a pastor.

But it is the healing which she found through the intercessory prayers of her parents and the grace of a loving God that she seeks to share with her clients.

"I know people can be healed of their hurts," she says. She encourages women not to "look back to yesterday and be robbed of tomorrow."

And to Christians, Lou's advice is pointed. "Get involved." She has little patience with Christians who say they are prolife and do little more than talk about it.

She offers practical words to them such as "Quit those looks and glances at single mothers with three unruly children in church. Go sit with her; offer to baby-sit, help her."

"Commit or quit talking," she says.

Independent Crisis Pregnancy Centers

In Chicago, Pregnancy Aid South Suburbs Assist Services has been open since 1982 to offer many of the same services offered by the extension centers modeled above. In 1995, the not-for-profit self-described "parachurch" group operated 3 centers in Chicago's south suburbs. The centers are under the umbrella of CareNet, the crisis pregnancy ministry of the Christian Action Council which was founded in 1975 by Dr. Harold O.J. Brown, with the advice and encouragement of Billy Graham and the late Francis A. Schaeffer.

While CareNet does not actually run the centers, the not-for-profit organization is available to give advice and gather legal information as well as be a prayer partner with the Chicago centers, according to Assist Services director Sue Davenger. Assist Services operates under a 13-member board of directors representing area churches.

The CareNet international office in Sterling, Virginia, produces educational materials and provides ongoing training for center board members, directors, and volunteers in more than 450 pregnancy care centers across the country. The 3 Chicago Pregnancy Aid South Suburbs Assist Services centers are among the most successful, according to CareNet officials.

In 1995, the 3 centers ministered to 1,828 girls and women aged 15 to 50. Most services are volunteer-driven. Some 65 volunteer counselors assist six full-time and five part-time staff.

In 1995, 1 center was open 40 hours per week; the second, 25; the third, 17. In 1995, of the clients who came for pregnancy tests, 502 tested positive. Of those clients, 342 chose to carry their babies to term, 32 chose to abort and stayed with their decisions, while 136 left the center undecided about what to do, according to center records.

Other services include counseling for the boyfriends of the women who come to the center. This service began in 1993 in response to the recognition that many of the boyfriends of center clients pressured their girlfriends to have an abortion. A volunteer male counselor works with the men. Additionally, joint counseling sessions are provided for the man and his girlfriend.

Prenatal programs run by volunteer registered nurses and postabortion support programs are a part of the center's ministry as well. The 3-year-old postabortion program run by the center's director of counseling seeks to examine life, offer hope, and introduce clients to Jesus and the restoration He offers, Sue says. "So many of the women are sealed away from a relationship with God," she says. "They live in a vacuum created by abortion."

In addition to center-based services, since 1992 Assist Services has offered abstinence education in public schools and churches through IMPACT. In 1995, a volunteer director and two paid part-time presenters took the IMPACT program to 18 high schools, 6 junior high schools, and 16 church groups. Twenty-three of the 24 schools were public schools. More than 5,837 teens heard the presentations.

Donations from concerned individuals, local businesses, and a plethora of churches in the area brought the year's budget to $350,000. During 1995, Full Gospel, Assemblies of God, Baptist, Christian Reformed, Community, Evangelical Free, Lutheran, Nazarene, Reformed, and Independent churches made financial contributions.

For Sue, it is the grassroots outreach to those with "no idea of the Lord" that draws her to crisis pregnancy ministry. Assist Services staff members, while very sensitive to the real and pressing need which draws the girls and women to the center, are unashamedly evangelistic. "We don't bombard them with the gospel or neglect their need or do anything to close the door to ministry," Sue says. But they do present the gospel in some fashion to each client. The presentation varies in intensity from mentioning the Bible or salvation through Jesus Christ to introducing a client to Who Jesus is to "just being able to give a card with the steps to salvation" to a client, Sue says. "You never know what God can do, even if someone refuses," she believes. In 1995, in the 3 centers, the gospel was presented in some fashion 1,640 times, resulting in 28 women who prayed to receive Christ on first hearing the gospel.

Put Your Faith to Work

Some ministry opportunities in crisis pregnancy ministry or ministry to unmarried mothers-to-be/mothers require specialized training while others only need a willing, compassionate Christian.

(These ideas require minimal time involvement and may serve as entry points for ministry to unmarried mothers-to-be/mothers or as onetime ministry projects.)

•Answer the phone.
•Do housekeeping chores.
•Shop yard sales and thrift shops for maternity and baby-care items.
•Repair and launder baby-care and maternity clothes.
•Work in a clothes room.
•Work with local businesses to secure donations of diapers, toiletries, etc., to distribute to clients.
•Provide transportation for clients referred for medical care.
•Staff a crisis pregnancy hot line. First, secure training.

(These ideas require a significant investment of time and a deep commitment to crisis pregnancy ministry.)

•Share your home with a pregnant unmarried girl or woman.
•Share your home with an unmarried woman and her baby.
•Become a foster parent. Check with religious and secular child-care agencies in your area for details.
•Adopt a child.

Selected Resources for Crisis Pregnancy Ministry

Alcorn, Randy. *Pro Life Answers to Pro Choice Arguments.* Portland, OR: Multnomah Press, 1992. An easy-to-use reference book which presents answers to the most frequently used prochoice arguments.

Boothe, Sylvia. *No Easy Choices* (The Dilemma of Crisis Pregnancy). Birmingham, AL: New Hope, 1990.

CareNet, A Ministry of the Christian Action Council, Materials List and Order Form. A 7-page list of, resources available from CareNet, 109 Carpenter Drive, Suite 100, Sterling, VA 20164; (703) 478-5661.

Garland, Diana. *Precious in His Sight* (A Guide to Child Advocacy), 2d. ed. Birmingham, AL: New Hope, 1996.

Life. What a Beautiful Choice. A 32-page resource list available from the Arthur S. DeMoss Foundation, P. O. Box 700, Valley Forge, PA 19482-0700.

Help, I'm Pregnant. A 14-minute video introducing the concept of crisis pregnancy centers. Alpharetta, GA: Home Mission Board; 1 (800) 634-2642.

Pierson, Anne, and Carol Risser. *Fifty-two Simple Things You Can Do to Be Pro-Life.* Minneapolis: Bethany House, 1990. Ways to speak up for life.

Stanford-Rue, Susan M., PhD. *Will I Cry Tomorrow? Healing Post-Abortion Trauma.* Old Tappan, NJ: Fleming H. Revell Company, 1986. In this poignant story of her own abortion experience, Stanford-Rue offers hope to women who have had abortions and helps counselors understand their pain.

Taylor, Laurie. *How Could This Happen?* Birmingham, AL: World Changers Resources, 1992.

Selected Ministries

Crisis Pregnancy Ministries
Alternatives to Abortion Ministries, Home Mission Board, 4200 North Point Parkway, Alpharetta, GA 30202; (770) 410-6000. Offers training and resources to churches nationwide.

Bethany Christian Services, Inc., 901 Eastern Avenue, NE, Grand Rapids, MI 49503-1295; (616) 459-6273. A national organization whose services include crisis pregnancy and family counseling, infant foster care placement, adoption, and maternity and shepherding homes.

Birthright, 686 North Broad Street, Woodbury, NJ 08096; (609) 848-1819 or 1 (800) 848-LOVE. Over 600 chapters across the country operate crisis pregnancy centers. All chapters are private and interdenominational.

CareNet, 109 Carpenter Drive, Suite 100, Sterling, VA 20164; (703) 478-5661. An agency of the Christian Action Council. Over 450 crisis pregnancy centers nationwide. Offers many resources.

Postabortion Healing
Open ARMS, P. O. Box 1056, Columbia, MO 65205; (314) 449-7672. Encourages those who have been involved in an abortion to face the experience and begin the process

of healing. Also provides counselor training using local resources and materials.

Project Rachel, c/o Respect Life Office, Archdiocese of Milwaukee, P. O. Box 2018, Milwaukee, WI 53201; (414) 483-4141. Sponsored by the Catholic Church but open to all faiths. Offers a network of resources for healing for those who have been involved in an abortion.

Women Exploited by Abortion (WEBA), Route 1, Box 821, Venus, TX 76084; (214) 366-3600. An international Christian organization for women who have had abortions. Offers one-on-one counseling and support groups.

General
National Right to Life Committee, 419 Seventh Street, NW, Suite 500, Washington, DC 20004-2293; (202) 626-8800.

For a more complete listing, consult *Life. What a Beautiful Choice,* a 32-page resource available from the Arthur S. DeMoss Foundation, P. O. Box 700, Valley Forge, PA 19482-0700.

Two Who Chose Life

Susan's Story
When Susan (not her real name) walked out the doors of the crisis pregnancy center (CPC) in Euliss, Texas, the volunteers who had talked with her could not predict what she would do.

She had already had one abortion. And although she had prayed to receive Christ on this visit to the CPC, the volunteers weren't sure of the depth of her words.

Susan didn't have an abortion. Instead, she came back to the center for help with medical costs and carried her baby to term. After the baby was born, the CPC lost touch with Susan.

One day, out of the blue, she called. She said she was back in town with her little son. She had no place to live, no idea about how to care for her baby or herself. She was staying at a Salvation Army shelter.

Center personnel helped her get out of the shelter. They helped her earn her high school equivalency and get a grant to attend a community college. With the help of a social worker, they found housing for her.

Susan began studying the Bible. She made a profession of faith in Jesus Christ and was baptized into a church.

Not only did she choose life for her son, she chose eternal life.

Sue's Story

One spring day, a 17-year-old African-American girl saw a billboard in Columbia, South Carolina, advertising Shiphrah Ministries. She called the number listed and talked with director Harriet Dial.

As God would have it, Harriet was scheduled to be in Columbia the next day. She arranged to meet Sue (not her real name) on a particular street corner.

To Harriet's surprise, the next day Sue was waiting for her, waiting to tell her story.

Sue's mother had left home when Sue was 8. To escape an abusive father, Sue ran away at 15. For 2 years, she lived on the streets, often indulging in alcohol and drugs. And now, at 17, she was pregnant, the result of gang rape.

"I told Sue if she wanted to change her life, she now had the opportunity, but it was up to her," Harriet says.

Sue agreed to go to Shiphrah. In six weeks, she had earned her GED. She made a profession of faith in Jesus and was baptized in the local Baptist church. In December, she gave birth to her baby and placed it for adoption with a Pennsylvania couple. And, with the help of the Shiphrah staff, she enrolled in a Christian college in Georgia for the spring semester.

"The Lord changes lives," Harriet says. "And He has provided this place where girls like Sue can let Him work."

74

Shattering the Myths

MYTH. Most unwed mothers are minorities.

FACT. Sixty (60) percent of births outside marriage in 1993 were to Anglo women.

MYTH. Most unwed mothers are teens.

FACT. Seventy (70) percent of births outside marriage in 1993 were to women older than 20.

In the United States:

•Ninety-eight (98) percent of abortions in the United States are for convenience.

•One in 3 women has had an abortion.

•One in 4 women involved in church has had an abortion.

•In 1993, 70 percent of births outside marriage were to women older than 20.

•In 1993, 60 percent of births outside marriage in the United States were to Anglo women.

•Over 1.1 million teenaged girls become pregnant each year—1 in 9.

•Every day 29 girls under age 15 give birth.

•Ten (10) percent of teen pregnancies lead to marriage while 50 percent end in abortion.

•More than 40 percent of teen pregnancies result in teenaged girls becoming parents.

•Four (4) percent of the babies born to teen mothers are placed for adoption.

Source: Alan Guttmacher Institute

What Scripture says about the value of life
Proverbs 24:11–12   Exodus 1:6–21
Exodus 20:13   Leviticus 19:16*b*
Isaiah 58:6–9

Unto the Least of These

Those who are successful in ministering in a crisis pregnancy center:
•Show unconditional love. No holier-than-thou attitude. Learn to hate the sin and love the sinner.
•Don't get caught up in the results.
•Have a strong sense of call.
•Are willing to get involved beyond the immediate problem.

Notes
[1]Sylvia Boothe, *No Easy Choices* (The Dilemma of Crisis Pregnancy) (Birmingham, AL: New Hope, 1990), 7.
[2]"Abortions, Teen Pregnancies Decline," *Louisville (Ky.) Western Recorder,* n.d.
[3]Ibid.
[4]"Religious Commitment Affects View on Abortion," *Louisville (Ky.) Western Recorder,* June 8, 1993, 1.
[5]Ibid.
[6]Boothe, *No Easy Choices,* 8.
[7]Ibid., cover 4.
[8]Kay Coles James with David Kuo, *Transforming America from the Inside Out* (Grand Rapids: Zondervan Publishing House, 1995), 108.
[9]"Ten Steps to Establishing a Crisis Pregnancy Center," *How to Establish a Crisis Pregnancy Center, a Manual* (Atlanta: Home Mission Board, n.d.), 4:1.
[10]Margaret L. Usdansky, "Single Motherhood: Stereotypes vs. Statistics," *New York Times,* February 11, 1996, 4.
[11]Ibid.
[12]Ibid.

O Lord, I'm glad you can
hear me in my own language.
I live in this strange country,
this place called the United States,
but I still can't understand this English.
Thanks, Lord, for letting me speak
my language when I talk to you.
One day.
I go to the grocery, I can't read
the labels on the cans and boxes.
I go to the doctor, but she can't
understand how I hurt.
My neighbor speaks to me, but all
I can say is "Hello. How are
you?"
If only tomorrow I could speak English.
Then tomorrow wouldn't have to
be like today.

—Joyce Sweeney Martin

"The success of any literacy missions
ministry is directly related to the amount
of time that is invested in prayer."
—Kendale Moore

4

Teaching Others to Read

If you can read this chapter, you can do something 27 million adult Americans cannot do. You can read. Put bluntly, those 27 million Americans are functional non-readers. Each year, the ranks of the nation's illiterate grow by an estimated 2.3 million, including newcomers from abroad. In addition, some 40 million more adults are considered barely competent in literacy skills, and that number is growing too. Many are among the nearly 1 million high school students who drop out of school each year.[1] When all is said and done, about 20 percent of adults—1 in 5—can't read, write, or reason well enough to compete in today's economy, according to a 1995 report from the United States Department of Education.[2] They cannot read a newspaper, a cookbook, the labels on food items, instruction manuals, or the Bible. They cannot read well enough to complete a job application or follow instructions on medicines. Another 34 percent are only marginally literate.[3]

While illiteracy may not be as visible as some other impairments, the consequences are devastating. On average, an illiterate adult earns 42 percent less than a literate high school graduate.[4] It is estimated that the cost of illiteracy to business and the taxpayer is $20 billion per year.[5] About 60 percent of the United States prison population is illiterate and 85 percent of all juvenile offenders have problems reading.[6]

And, as the reading level necessary to function in an ever-increasing technological society continues to rise, literacy experts say illiteracy is not likely to be eradicated soon. Today, 40 percent of all current jobs require limited skills, but it is estimated that only 27 percent of newly created jobs fall into the low-skill categories.[7]

Over the past two decades, literacy programs have sprung up across the country. Community-based programs housed in such places as community colleges and public libraries as well as church-based programs have tackled the problem of illiteracy. But, according to literacy experts, all the programs combined fill only about 10 percent of the need.[8]

On the church scene, most religious denominations strongly encourage their members to become involved in community-based literacy work, but only a few groups advocate literacy as a missions outreach of a local church. The most comprehensive literacy-as-missions model has been developed by the Southern Baptist Convention. For over 20 years, the denomination's Home Mission Board has sponsored intensive workshops to train literacy leaders. Each summer literacy ministry volunteers from across the country have been trained to return home to train other literacy leaders, thus multiplying the ministry.

"Witnessing to the gospel of Jesus Christ through meeting the needs of adults who are functional nonreaders, people who need to learn to speak English, and school-age children and youth who need help with school" is the upfront, stated goal and guiding philosophy of the Southern Baptist Convention literacy missions ministry program.[9]

"We don't do literacy work, but we do literacy missions work," says Kendale Moore, director of literacy missions for the Southern Baptist Home Mission Board. He is quick to acknowledge the value of community-based literacy programs and he encourages Southern Baptist churches to join local literacy coalitions. He believes there are big differences, however, in church-based and community-based programs.

"Church-based literacy missions ministry is a way to respond personally to the gospel and to introduce Jesus Christ to people," Kendale says. "Community-based groups exist to meet the literacy needs of the community."

Kendale believes church-based literacy ministries offer something unique. Distinctive features of church-based literacy-as-ministry programs are:

•Volunteers are enlisted from the church's membership; they have accepted Christ as personal Savior. They feel a sense of mission or call from God to this ministry.

•Volunteers are trained not only to use appropriate teaching materials and to relate to students but also to tell the students about Jesus. They are trained to use the Bible as a resource. Each lesson incorporates a Scripture portion to reinforce the reading concept taught in the textbook. Volunteers always tell their students up front how Scripture will be used. "If someone says he doesn't want to read the Scripture, we ask him to come to a couple of sessions and see how the Scripture is used," Kendale says. When the students see it is not a "pushing down the throat," most respond favorably.

•The ministry receives funding from the church or group of churches. It takes no money from the government. The ministry is approved by the church as a bona fide program just like Sunday School or any other ministry program.

•The three components of Southern Baptist literacy missions ministries are modeled in this chapter: adult reading and writing (ARW); conversational English (CE); and tutoring children and youth (TCY). While the TCY component is less than 4 years old, it is the fastest growing.

Literacy Missions Definitions

Adult Reading and Writing (ARW)—Ministry to English-speaking (usually American-born) adults who are functionally illiterate. The ARW leader workshop requires 16 hours of training.

Conversational English (CE)—Ministry to non-English-speaking adults wanting to learn English as a second language (ESL). While conversation is the primary skill taught, reading and writing in English is also included. The CE leader workshop requires 16 hours of training.

Tutoring Children and Youth (TCY)—Ministry to help school-age children who are having difficulty with their schoolwork. The TCY leader workshop requires 14 hours of training.

To qualify to attend ARW, CE, or TCY workshops, a tutor must have completed a basic 16-hour training course and have eight months experience as a literacy volunteer. The basic course is offered in Southern Baptist-sponsored workshops in most states. Contact the Literacy Missions Department, Home Mission Board, 4200 North Point Parkway, Alpharetta, GA 30302; (770) 410-6445.

Adult Reading and Writing in Georgia

The young single mother of two children just never seemed to be able to get to her tutoring sessions on time. She was either too early or very late. Then her tutor found out why: she couldn't tell time.

The young man was about to lose his job as a mechanic because he couldn't read the automobile manuals.

A 21-year-old man wanted to attend church with his girlfriend, but was intimidated by the "place of the books"—the Bible and hymnbooks.

She helped her athlete boyfriend make it through his high school academic courses, coaching him through each step. He graduated, but he could not read. Now he was her husband and the father of her children; but because he could not read, he could not adequately support his family. "I helped him get his diploma," she said. "But I can't go to work with him."

Hopeless situations? No. Thankfully, each of these people lived in or around Blairsville, Georgia, where for more than 15 years, some caring Christians have been involved in helping adults learn to read and write.

In the name of Jesus, these Christians have shown the depth of their faith by their works. Guided by the words of Jesus recorded in Luke 4:18, they have worked to help those who can't read "recover their sight," says Renva Acree, who has spearheaded the ministry from its inception.

Renva's own eyes had to be opened to the need for literacy missions. Although she had been very active in the Southern Baptist Woman's Missionary Union for many years, she says somehow she had missed literacy missions.

Devotional messages given by a longtime literacy missions advocate at a ministers' wives retreat in the summer of 1979 helped her see the need. Mary Alred laced each devotional with illustrations from her literacy work.

"I cornered her and asked her to tell me more about literacy missions," Renva remembers. Mary suggested Renva take training in literacy missions.

For Renva, it was a natural. During her 30 years as a schoolteacher she often had encountered parents of her students who could not read and write. She knew something was desperately wrong, but "didn't know I could help," she says. And as a Christian and a minister's wife, she felt the tug of the Spirit of God to do something.

God confirmed her mission the next summer when she and her husband attended a meeting in New Mexico. While registering for the conference, Renva noticed a sign-up sheet for anyone interested in taking a 16-hour literacy training workshop that week. She signed up.

Renva planned to quit her public school career in order to assist her husband with his work and begin a literacy ministry. But again, God had plans which would meld literacy needs with the desires of her heart to get involved in addressing illiteracy.

The county school superintendent asked her to become an itinerant behavior disorder teacher in a newly funded special education position. That opened the way not only for Renva to work with children from first grade through high school but also with their parents. When Renva asked the superintendent if she could develop a literacy program to use with high school nonreaders based on the literacy program she had learned in New Mexico, he agreed.

And, at about the same time, in the process of helping a first-grader, Renva met the young woman who would become her first adult student. "She's just like me. She'll never learn to read," the mother said as Renva worked with her little girl. When Renva asked if the single mother of two would like to learn to read, she said yes.

By 1982, Renva realized she needed to train other literacy workers in order to make a bigger dent in the literacy problem. She attended the annual National Literacy Workshop at Samford University in Birmingham, Alabama, where she received certification as a trainer. She returned to north Georgia with an expanded mission: train teachers. Soon, what had begun as a God-given mission to one person grew to encompass a multitude of volunteers from many denominations in a two-county area. Today, Presbyterians, Lutherans, Methodists, Roman Catholics, and Baptists serve as tutors in ARW and TCY in the Blairsville area.

In the Blairsville area, the ARW one-on-one ministry reaches:

•Adults in the community. While some students are found through public school parent-teacher conferences and others through ARW ads in local newspapers and flyers spread about town, Renva says word of mouth is the best advertisement. Since adult nonreaders are often reluctant to ask for help, a word from a friend who is learning to read carries a lot of weight. One man called to say he had learned his neighbor "had his own tutor," and then asked if he could have one too.

Renva is quick to point out that many adult nonreaders have learned to function well and are financially successful. She sees many in her area who grew up in the depression of the 1930s, who had to quit school to help their families survive, and who never returned to school. Now, they are nearing retirement, but still can't read.

Interestingly, these longtime residents have been joined in recent years by a large number of outsiders who have moved to the area to retire. Now, the two counties of Union and Towns rank number one and number three among Georgia's counties in the number of residents over the age of 65. And it is the retirees moving in who have become some of Renva's most avid literacy volunteers. Literacy is a "ready-made way" for them to be involved in missions, she says. Many can't fathom living all one's life without being able to read, so they are eager to help others learn how.

Tutors and students generally meet in the local library because in the winter it's the only warm building in town, Renva says. In many communities across the nation, churches are used for these sessions, but in Renva's community the churches are small and are unheated on weekdays.

Not all adults who want to work with a tutor stick out the entire program. One man wanted to learn to read and write in order to write a thank-you letter to the family who had reared him. He worked with a tutor for about a year, wrote his letter, and then quit the program.

•Adults in a sheltered workshop for the mentally and physically disabled. Very patient tutors work with all those who can benefit from their help, Renva says.

•Adult males incarcerated at a probation detention center for such things as repeated drinking under the influence (DUI) violations and nonpayment of child support. Tutors work with the men who range in age from 18 to 39 during the three to six months they live at the center. Renva finds most often the men are open and ready to make changes in their lives. Many have made professions of faith in Jesus Christ. When an inmate leaves the center, literacy volunteers put him in contact with a literacy ministry in the town where he will be living; if the town has no literacy work, they put him in touch with a church.

•Adults in the workplace. The state of Georgia gives a special tax break to factories with 50 or more employees whose employees will take advantage of literacy education. Currently, tutors are placed in two area factories.

•A support group for ARW volunteers. To combat the isolation inherent in working one-on-one, Renva founded two support groups for tutors. Each group meets once every two months for support and continuing education.

In a state where 38 to 39 percent of the population does not have a high school diploma, the need for ARW literacy missions is not going away anytime soon.

To Read and Write: A Classic Story

"And the Lord answered me, and said, Write the vision, and make it plain upon tables, that he may run that readeth it" (Hab. 2:2).

"Watching an adult learn to read is like turning a light on in a dark room. Next to becoming a Christian, learning to read is one of the most important life-changing events. For the Christian, learning to read the Bible opens vast opportunities for spiritual growth that otherwise are closed. The non-Christian reading the Bible for himself or herself enters a dimension of understanding that hearing alone does not give. Enabling a person to read is, indeed, enabling him to run."[10]

Almost 40 years ago, Kentuckian Lillian Isaacs began a literacy mission in Appalachia which still bears fruit today. Much of her story is chronicled in the book *So He May Run Who Reads,* from which the above paragraph is taken. Miss Lillian's account of how her first student, Ruth, learned to read is a classic which continues to inspire adult reading and writing ministries today.

My eyes scanned the Pineville, Ky., town square. "There they are!" I said to my husband, John. I pointed him in the direction of the pair waiting on the square near the curb. John stopped the car. Ruth and her teenaged grandson climbed in.

Ruth, a small, neatly dressed woman with work-worn hands, greeted us and settled in the backseat. As we headed out of town we could hear Ruth happily spelling and then pronouncing words of the passing signs: "C-U-R-V-E," she'd say, "curve. . . ."

I turned around. Ruth sat perfectly erect, a little smile on her face. "Today, I'm sittin' and ridin' instead of standin' and ironin'—and just because I can read."

We were en route to the [Baptist] Mountain Preacher's Bible Conference in Oneida, [Kentucky]. Pretty soon I could hear Ruth rehearsing the testimony she had prepared for the meeting: "I'm the oldest of nine children," she began, her voice jolting with the bumps in the road. "The year I started school, the foot log washed out. My parents hoped I could go to school the next year. But by then there was a baby. Mama needed me to help.

"As the years rolled by, the other children all went to school. But Mama always needed me: to tend babies, to wash, to cook.

"I wanted to go to school to learn to read. But when I finally could go, I was too old to sit with the little first-graders." Ruth paused. She looked through the car window at the trees and mountains skimming past. Ruth seemed to reflect a moment, then continued.

"Always in my heart I wanted to know how to read. But when I'd look at the other children's books, I couldn't read—not even the primers.

"At an early age I married. Then I had babies of my own. When my children were old enough to read, I would look at their books and wish I could read, too."

Ruth explained that as she grew up, she made three requests of the Lord. And over the years she watched for his answers. "God is good," she said. "He heered my prayers."

Her first prayer was for God to send a preacher who would tell her how to be saved. "You know I heered a heap of preachin' before I heered how to be saved."

I interrupted Ruth: "Be sure to tell the preachers that when you talk to them today." Ruth shifted in the backseat. Then she said to me, "You remember it was just a year ago when you came to the missionary meeting at Ethyl's? You asked the ladies to learn how to teach folks like me to read." Her eyes filled with tears. "The Lord says to me, 'Ruth, that's for you. Listen.'"

"I was on the back porch listening as I ironed. For years I had prayed to learn how to read the Bible. My second big prayer was about to be answered. That afternoon after everyone left, I went to Ethyl and asked, 'When are you goin' to learn me to read?'"

"You know, Ethyl was dumbfounded. She told me, 'I didn't know you couldn't read. You never told me. Why didn't you tell me you couldn't read?' I answered her, 'Why should I say anything? Nobody was going to do anything about it, anyway.'"

We were approaching Oneida.

"Ruth, can you describe what learning to read means to you?" I asked.

She nodded. "At night I don't sleep well. You know my husband and daughter lay sick for years, so during that time I didn't go to bed. Since they died, I have trouble sleeping. But I don't mind, now, I tell myself, 'Ruth, you can read.' I just reach up over my bed and turn on the light.

"Some nights I read 'til two o'clock in the morning."

Then she told me, "My third prayer is that God will let me read this Book from kiver to kiver." She thumbed through the pages of the Bible in her lap. "Today," she said, "I'm going to read part of the third chapter of John."

As I thought about Ruth's words, I realized anew how God longs to communicate with His children. Jesus is referred to as the Word: "In the beginning was the Word, and the Word was with God and the Word was God. . . .

And the Word was made flesh and dwelt among us (and we beheld His glory, the glory as of the only begotten of the Father) full of grace and truth" (John 1:1,14). Literacy missions, I thought, must be born in the heart of God.

That day, Ruth stood before the conference of pastors: "There is nothing like reading. Reading makes shopping easy; I can read street signs, read my mail, read the newspaper. But most of all I can read my Bible," Ruth told them.

"After God saved me, I prayed he would learn me to read his Word." Ruth smiled as she opened her Bible. "I want to read part of my favorite chapter, John 3." As she read, Ruth's words came slowly. When she got to the word "condemnation," syllable by syllable she spelled and pronounced it: "c-o-n—con, d-e-m—dem, n-a-t-i-o-n. That condemnation word," she said, "gives me a little trouble. But I know what it means."

"There is nothing like reading," she told the group. "I thank God that I have learned to read. I thank him for Ethyl who taught me. I thank Him for the day Mrs. Isaacs asked the ladies to take the workshop [to learn to teach adults to read]. Are you thankful you can read?"

As Ruth spoke, many wept. Later, Ruth, John, George, and I ate dinner in the school dining room. Food passed around the table, but Ruth's plate remained empty. "Take some food," I offered. Ruth shook her head. "No, I can't eat," she insisted. "Aren't you hungry?" I asked.

Ruth admitted she was, but explained. "I can't eat today. This is the first time in my life I'm being waited on at a table instead of doin' the waiting on—just because I can read." Ruth leaned forward. "This is a sacred hour," she said, solemnly.[11]

Conversational English in California

"When the Lord called me to missions, He just called me to go back home and minister there," June Tate says. Ironically, for the woman who wanted to "go into the world" with the gospel, that call to go home has put her up close with people from around the world. Home for June is Orange County, California. And missions is teaching English to the foreign born.

Conversational English as ministry has been June's passion for more than 25 years. She read an article in a missions magazine about ethnics who needed to learn to speak English, and that prompted her to attend a literacy awareness workshop in New Mexico. That, in turn, prompted her to take English as second language (ESL) and CE training at a local library when she returned home.

Soon thereafter, June began working with her first students—the Robert Dehoop family from Argentina who had come to the States to do church-related work. Each Friday night for the next 4 years, at her home or theirs, June and the Argentines gathered around the dining room table to study. June's engineer husband, Burney, often joined in to baby-sit the Argentines' young children.

Within a few months after she met the Argentines, June and a friend began ESL classes at their church. In preparation for the first class, they handed out announcements across the street from their town's high school. They hoped to enlist one student each. Instead, 30 students showed up on the first night of class. Within a few months, the ministry had grown to the point that the church began a Sunday School class in Spanish with 10 Hispanics in attendance. That class eventually became a self-supporting Spanish church with one of June's first students (Robert Dehoop) as pastor.

A few years later, when at the end of the Vietnam Conflict, Southeast Asians were sent by the United States government to nearby Camp Pendleton, June once again got involved in literacy missions. Twice a week, she accompanied a Southern Baptist missionary to the military base to assist with ESL classes.

After a few years' break, June returned to literacy missions about 6 years ago. Since then, she has served as literacy coordinator for the California Southern Baptist

Convention. She teaches literacy workshops, speaks on literacy needs, and seeks to broaden the base of literacy missions in her state. With California's growing ethnicity, it is a mission which will keep June busy for many years to come.

Conversational English in New York

Kim (not her real name) works from 7:00 A.M. to 7:00 P.M. seven days a week in one of the 500 garment factories in the heart of Manhattan's Chinatown. Since she is paid by the piece, she is lucky if she makes $5 an hour with no overtime and no benefits.

At night, she goes home to a two-bedroom apartment which she shares with 30 other people. They sleep two to a single bed in eight-hour shifts. And, together, they pay $2,000 a month rent.

Kim is not alone. More than 30,000 Chinese work in Chinatown's garment center. Most are women. While some of the factories are well run, many are little better than the notorious sweatshops of yesteryear. In 1995, as many as 100,000 new immigrants came into Chinatown, hoping to better their lives. Instead, they often have found unbearable conditions. One Chinese pastor who ministers in Chinatown estimates that 60 percent would go back to China if they could.

Finding a way to bring the gospel of Jesus Christ into such circumstances has not been easy. Less than 5 percent of the Chinese workers are Christians, but many are eager to learn about Christianity as a part of American culture. Many of the younger women in particular are interested in learning English, but they have little time left over after working long hours.

Pastor Sam Lai of Trust in God Church in Chinatown envisioned taking ESL to them in the factories. When a church member opened his two garment factories for the classes, Pastor Lai knew he had an open door not only to meet the literacy needs of the workers, but also to share the Christian faith and "to invite them to accept Jesus as their personal Savior and to go to church," he said. But he had no volunteers. He called the Metropolitan New York Baptist Association (Southern Baptist) to which his church belongs and asked for help.

Now, once a week, literacy missions ministry volunteers spend the lunch hour teaching Conversational English in the factory. The women gather in three small groups; sometimes they pull up a table and sit down in the middle of the fray, sometimes they stand up. Some weeks, class is preempted by a rush work order. Most weeks, actual teaching time is about 35 minutes. The women are eager to learn and are appreciative of the classes; and they are open to the gospel, Rebecca Waugh, who coordinates the effort, says. Christian holidays such as Easter and Christmas provide natural entrees to talk about Jesus, she adds.

While the ministry is in its infancy and is only a drop in the bucket of needs in Chinatown, the volunteers have high hopes of beginning more classes on other floors of the two factories where they now work and of moving on to other factories as well. Rebecca dreams of involving all 24 of Chinatown's Chinese churches in an interdenominational literacy ministry in Chinatown. She dreams of the day when midday in Chinatown will be synonymous with literacy missions ministry classes.

Learning to Speak English: One Woman's Story

Natasha (not her real name) was born and reared in Czechoslovakia. In her native country she was a grammar school teacher. She speaks Russian, Slovak, Yogoslav, and—now—English.

But when Natasha came to Detroit, Michigan, in 1970, she spoke only a little English. She says, "In my country I was educated. I was a teacher. In America, I felt stupid. I wouldn't speak to anyone, not even my neighbors. I didn't want them to know how I talk. I was very lonely. For 3 years, we lived in the city of Detroit. Then we moved to a suburb. And I was still lonely. For another 5 years, I was lonely. I cried almost every day.

"Then one day in 1978, new neighbors moved across the street. They had moved from California to work at the church next door to where I lived. Even as the moving van was being unloaded, the lady of the house spoke to me. She said, 'Hi, I'm Marsha (not her real name). I'm your new neighbor.'"

From that moment, things began to change for Natasha. Marsha talked with her, accepting her faltering English, and forcing her to improve even as they talked. Marsha helped Natasha regain her confidence in her intellectual and social abilities. She helped her learn to drive a car. And then Marsha talked to Natasha about Jesus. She even encouraged Natasha to become involved in a neighborhood Bible study led by the pastor's wife at the church next door.

It's been almost 20 years since that moving van arrived. Marsha and her family have moved away. But Marsha's caring is still reaping results. Natasha became a Christian in 1981. One of her sons has worked as a volunteer missionary in another state, and the entire family has been enriched because Marsha cared enough to help them adjust to their life in the United States.

Tutoring Children and Youth

Each Wednesday, around 5:00 P.M., two buses pull out of the parking lot at First Baptist Church on Perry Street and drive two miles to the Tulane Court public housing community in Montgomery, Alabama. Seventy or more children eagerly board the buses, ready for an evening of one-on-one tutoring at two area churches. One bus drops children at First Baptist, while the other goes to Hutchinson Street Missionary Baptist Church.

Each Wednesday, across Montgomery, this scene is repeated as more than 400 children from the city's seven public housing communities fan out to 24 of the city's churches. The children join in each church's family night meal and then spend 45 minutes in one-on-one time with their tutors. After a brief devotional/Bible story, the children ride the buses home.

The highly successful TCY program, which is in its seventh year, rarely has absentees. In fact, sometimes children who are not registered for the program jump on the bus because they want to attend too. The program is one segment of STEP (Strategies to Elevate People) a national program which began in the 1970s in Harlem to assist inner-city churches in their work with the poor of their communities.

Montgomery churches got involved in STEP in 1986 when some of the city's religious leaders met to discuss ways to minister to the poor and to present the gospel to them, according to Lee Baugh, executive director of the Montgomery program. Tutoring Children and Youth is just one aspect of the STEP program in Montgomery.

Beginning with 7 member churches working in one public housing community, the STEP group has grown to include 24 congregations working in all of Montgomery's seven housing communities. These churches represent Baptist (Southern, National, and National Baptists dually aligned with American Baptists), Presbyterian, Methodist, Seventh Day Adventist, and Church of Christ. The $97,000 annual budget comes from individuals, churches, civic groups, and a few small grants. No government money is accepted in order not to compromise the strong spiritual dimension of the program. In-kind services are estimated at $350,000 annually.

STEP personnel work closely with the elementary and junior high schools near each housing community. Teachers recommend students who need extra help, parental permission is secured, and students register in August for the year-long program.

Ideally, an African-American church and an Anglo church are paired to work with one public housing community. For example, Hutchinson Street Missionary Baptist

Church, a National Baptist church, is paired with First Baptist Church on Perry Street, a Southern Baptist congregation, to work with the 650-unit Tulane Court housing development.

While the program operates under the STEP umbrella, each church is free to make adaptations, according to Jane Ferguson, director of First Baptist's program. For example, Dexter Avenue King Memorial Church takes boys only, and their tutors incorporate a lot of biblical memory work in their program.

Volunteers are the heart of the ministry. Some volunteers are schoolteachers or college professors; some are attorneys; some are housewives; some are students at nearby Huntington College. One is a fighter pilot. But the vocational or educational background is not the deciding factor in a successful volunteer-tutor relationship. Success comes when a tutor cares about more than tutoring; success comes when a tutor cares about the child. Not only does a child find in a caring tutor someone who will give undivided attention but also someone to whom the child is accountable. For a child who never hears school mentioned at home or for a child whose parents would like to help, but don't know how, this becomes a stabilizing factor.

Involvement with the student's family is also key. "Tutoring opens the door," Morgan Simpson, a professor of education at the Auburn University at Montgomery, says. He directs the program at Carriage Hills Church of Christ. Often, tutors at his church get involved in assisting students' families needing emergency help. Once, a Carriage Hills family provided a temporary home for a young girl whose family moved off and left her. Another time, when a tutor moved out of state, her student dropped out of the program and would not come back. Finally, the student wrote her former tutor to say her family was about to be evicted from their apartment. The tutor wrote Carriage Hills, and the church arranged to pay electric bills so the family would not be evicted. The student reentered the tutoring program.

Sometimes Carriage Hills tutors go to the Smiley Court community to meet the students' parents. "The first time in the projects [located 15 miles away from their church], many tutors are nervous and concerned," Simpson says. They believe "all the things the media has said" about such communities, he says. But once they go to Smiley Court, they find out "there are more good people out there than bad."

First Baptist, Hutchinson Street Missionary, and Carriage Hills maintain year-round ministries to the children and their families. First Baptist and Hutchinson Street Missionary Church team up to offer a weekly support group for single mothers and a performing arts group to teach children voice and piano. Carriage Hills takes the children on field trips and sends some of them to summer camp.

At all 24 locations, the tutoring program has a strong spiritual element. While tutors do not buttonhole the children, they do find it natural to talk about church and about Christ. Each year, several children pray to receive Christ.

In March 1995, a more direct evangelism program spun off the tutoring ministry. A door-to-door evangelism effort was started after some Christians in the project asked for it. "Older Christians know one of the answers to the drugs in the projects is a personal relationship with Jesus," Lee believes. To date, from that door-to-door visitation, six Bible studies with 12 people in three housing communities have been started.

During one time period, Carriage Hills members went to Smiley Court each Thursday night to lead devotions for the children. Does the tutoring program work? Jane, Lee, and Morgan say a resounding "Yes," but they caution that long-term commitment is essential. Too often, they say, do-gooders who don't last do more harm than good. "Long-term commitment isn't easy," Morgan says. "But you win in the long run."

The Joy of Tutoring: One Woman's Story
Rhonda Shearer is a tutor in the STEP program in Montgomery, Alabama. Following, in her own words, are excerpts from a letter she wrote about her experiences.

"I have had the opportunity to work with a disadvantaged student for the last two years. When I began to tutor her, my student was in the sixth grade for the second time, she was failing most of her subjects and receiving the worst possible marks in conduct. She also had been suspended repeatedly.

"Initially at tutoring, she was hostile, uncooperative, and disruptive. She refused to bring her homework. Gradually, she opened up about her abusive home life, brothers in prison, and teen sisters with babies who encouraged her (at age 13) to have a child so the family could receive more government assistance, etc.

"After a few months, she seemed to understand that she had been accepted in spite of her background. I guess a rapport had been established. She became open to efforts at self-improvement in education and behavior. As a result, she passed the sixth grade.

"She is now a seventh-grader who has passing marks in all of her subjects. She has vastly improved her marks in conduct and she has become involved in extracurricular activities.

"At tutoring, her improvement has been phenomenal. She is obedient, she brings her homework, and she seems to have a smile for everyone. She seems secure in knowing there is someone here who cares about her and how she lives her young life."

Put Your Faith to Work

Kendale Moore, director of literacy missions ministries at the Home Mission Board, suggests ten steps for beginning an ARW, CE, or TCY tutoring ministry:

1. Vote to recognize the ministry as a part of the church(es) programming.
2. Select a director or chairperson for the ministry.
3. Enlist teachers and other workers.
4. Provide training for teachers.
5. Provide encouragement and support for the teachers.
6. Secure funding.
7. Enlist students.
8. Place students with teachers.
9. Provide prayer support.
10. Continue to inform sponsoring churches or groups of churches.

Ways to Get Involved in Literacy Ministry

(These ideas require minimal time involvement and may serve as entry points to literacy missions.)

•Baby-sit children of students involved in CE or ARW.
•Baby-sit children of literacy volunteers.
•Provide refreshments for literacy missions groups.
•Provide refreshments for support groups for literacy missions volunteers.
•Provide financial assistance for transportation costs for literacy missions volunteers.
•Provide a scholarship for a literacy missions volunteer to attend a continuing education workshop.
•Provide transportation and/or child care to adult high school dropouts so they can return to school.

Biblical Insights on the Importance of Literacy

Acts 8:26–35	John 1:1,14
Luke 4:14–21	Habakkuk 2:2

How to Share Your Faith with a Literacy Student

•Share your personal Christian experience and testimony. As a part of training, literacy missions volunteers learn how to give a two-minute testimony.
•Pray with and for your student.
•Use the Bible as teaching material.
•Demonstrate the fruit of the spirit while teaching: love, joy, peace, patience, kindness, goodness, faithfulness, gentleness, self-control.
•Provide Scriptures and Christian reading material for your student.
•Invite your student to church services and activities.
•Provide support and encouragement for your student during times of personal celebration and crisis.

Qualifications of a Literacy Missions Volunteer

•A sense of mission or call from God to this ministry.
•Ability to read and write English.
•Completion of a 16-hour literacy missions training workshop.
•Commitment to teach once a week for at least six months. Most sessions last 1½ to 2 hours.

Responsibilities of a Literacy Missions Volunteer

•Pray for and with each student.
•Prepare lessons based on workshop training.
•Keep records of students' progress.
•Teach at least once a week.
•Attend monthly teachers meetings.
•Contact students when they are absent.
•Commit to share your faith and testimony with students.

Selected Resources for Literacy Ministries

Alford, Richard. *Tutoring Youth.* A manual developed by Alford who is a tutor at First Baptist Church, Montgomery, Alabama. For more information, contact First Baptist Church, 305 South Perry Street, Montgomery, AL 36104.

Harris, Doris. *My Friend Can't Read.* Birmingham, AL: World Changers Resources, 1993. A booklet which suggests ways youth can help friends who have trouble reading.

Snowden, Mark, et al. *Meeting the World* (Ministering Cross-Culturally). Birmingham, AL: New Hope, 1992. Learn how to relate to various ethnic groups.

Various authors. *Making Wise Choices: Helping Children Understand Social and Moral Issues.* Birmingham, AL: New Hope, 1995. Includes illiteracy.

Available from Church and Community Ministries Department, Home Mission Board, 4200 North Point Parkway, Alpharetta, GA 30202; 1 (800) 634-2462:

Brochures
Help! I'm Drowning in a Sea of Words!!
Literacy Missions. How to begin a literacy missions ministry.
How to Prepare for a Literacy Missions Workshop
Local Church Literacy Missions Needs Survey

Videos
Like Lighting a Candle
That All May Read God's Word

Agencies

American Literacy Council, 680 Fort Washington Avenue, New York, NY 10040; (214) 781-0099.

Notes

[1]"Help! I'm Drowning in a Sea of Words!!" (Atlanta: Home Mission Board, December 1995).

[2]"Facts on Adult Literacy," US Commission on Literacy, as quoted from US Department of Education statistics, //www.libertynet. org:80, February 15, 1996.

[3]Ibid.

[4]"Facts on Adult Literacy," as quoted from *Laubach Literacy Action,* //www.libertynet. org:80, February 15, 1996.

[5]"Facts on Adult Literacy," as quoted from *United Way, Illiteracy: A National Crisis,* //www.libertynet.org:80, February 15, 1996.

[6]"Facts on Adult Literacy," as quoted from US Department of Education statistics, //www.libertynet.org:80, February 15, 1996.

[7]"Facts on Adult Literacy," as quoted from *Workforce 2000,* US Department of Labor, //www.libertynet.org:80, February 15, 1996.

[8]Kendale Moore, interview by author, December 7, 1995.

[9]Ibid.

[10]Mildred Blankenship and Lillian Isaacs, *So He May Run Who Reads* (Atlanta: Home Mission Board, 1984), 2.

[11]Ibid., 5–8.

I was well fed,
So I did not see the hungry child standing next to me.
Nor did I see the look of fear in the young mother's eyes
As she held the child near.
I had the means within my grasp.
I thought nothing of the anxious clasp of the old man's hands
As he faced a debt and thought of the funds he could not get.
I was not in bonds; I was free,
So I could self-righteously pass by the jail,
For I was good and did the things that a Christian should.
Yes, I went to Sunday School and church,
And I could turn my head from the stumbling lurch of the drunken man
As he fell in the gutter with a burden so great he could not utter it.
And so I went along my way, saw nothing but a sun-filled day,
And did good deeds.
I failed to see the very ones who needed me,
And when at last it was time for bed,
Dutifully, my prayers I said.
I tried in vain to go to sleep,
But a voice said sharply, "Feed My sheep!"
I heard someone call my name, and slowly to my vision
Came the child and the mother, hand in hand,
The frightened face of the tired old man,
The prison and the souls inside,
And the drunken man in the gutter.
I said: "O Lord, how can this be?
There were too many here for me."
And He replied gently,
"There is a way
With sufficiency to meet your day.
This is how it can be done:
You can feed them one by one."[1]
                              —Anonymous

"Americans spend more money on watches and jewelry than on federal food programs."

—David Beckmann, president, Bread for the World

5

$\mathscr{F}$eeding the Hungry

Americans say hunger in the United States is a serious problem, and we try to do something about it. In fact, we operate more than 150,000 private organizations to distribute food to the hungry; we pass out an estimated $3 billion to $4 billion worth of food each year through food banks, food pantries, and soup kitchens; and half of us make a financial contribution to hunger relief each year.[2]

And yet, according to the hunger advocacy group Bread for the World, "As a nation, we are further from a solution to hunger than we were fifteen years ago."[3]

Consider these statistics:
•At any given time, between 20 and 30 million Americans face hunger.[4]

One of every five children lives in poverty and sometimes goes hungry.[5] Child poverty reached its highest level in 30 years in 1994, according to the Children's Defense Fund, a Washington-based children's advocacy group. One in three children can expect to fall below the poverty line at some time before age 16. The poverty line for a family of three is an annual income of less than $12,590, according to the federal Department of Health and Human Services.[6]

•One in 10 Americans make use of food pantries, soup kitchens, and other food distribution programs, according to a March 1994 survey by Second Harvest, a nationwide network of food banks. That's 25 million Americans, nearly half of whom are under 17 years of age.[7]

•The face of hunger has changed. "It's no longer just the single man on the street. It's children, mothers, the newly unemployed, the working poor."[8]

According to Second Harvest, nearly one-third of the households making use of emergency food services have someone working full-time or part-time.[9]

Very few people deny the enormity or the scope of the hunger problem. But now, more than ever, the debate over hunger and other issues which affect the poor seems to center on whether the government should spend more to eradicate poverty or whether the government should spend less and let private charities—including churches—fill in the gap.

Groups like Bread for the World argue for a both-and approach. Bread for the World says that "US government policies [tax cuts, reduced social spending, and tolerating high unemployment levels] are partly to blame for the growth of hunger in the United States during the 1980s," and that "private charity needs to be complemented by stronger government efforts."[10] Bread for the World believes that hunger can be eradicated with a three-pronged approach: economic; political; and religious.

•Economic. Getting more results from "the billions of dollars and millions of volunteers already working to help the hungry."

•Political. The emergence of a major social movement in the vein of the civil rights and environmental movements to transform the politics of hunger.

•Religious. A "vision of God's movement in history" based on the Scriptures that say, "God hears the cries of the hungry and brings justice to bear."[11]

On the other hand, some people argue that pared-down aid to the poor will push them to escape poverty and its attendant hunger. They argue that in the long run, less help is more.

But, while the argument continues, there has been a quiet explosion of efforts to assist the poor and hungry at the grassroots level. Consider the statistics at the beginning of this chapter.

On the religious scene, faith communities have taken the lead in responding to hunger. More than 250,000 of the nation's local religious communities give to emergency hunger relief, and about 48 percent of congregations have food pantries, according to Bread for the World.[12] In many communities, such efforts are ecumenical and community-based.

Additionally, many ministries which began with a primary focus on hunger have branched out to address attendant issues. Three of these are modeled in this chapter. The Kitchen, Inc., a parish-based ministry in Springfield, Missouri, was begun by five Catholic sisters as a soup kitchen. Today, it offers a wide range of ministries aimed to break the cycle of poverty. At Metropolitan Baptist Church in Cambridge, Massachusetts, what began in the mid-1980s as a community meal provided by one, small local church has developed into a range of ministries, including an interdenominational economic development program through the Christian Economic Coalition of Boston. The Christian Economic Coalition is modeled also.

When Hunger Is Just the Tip of the Iceberg

When the five Little Portion Franciscan Sisters accepted their bishop's challenge to do something to help the needy in their city, they thought a small soup kitchen would be perfect. After all, most people in Springfield, Missouri, seemed to think there were few, if any, poor people among their residents.

On March 27, 1983, the sisters served the first meal from the kitchen of a parish elementary school. That first night, 30 people showed up to eat. By the end of the summer, more than 200 people regularly waited in line to receive the evening meal.

It didn't take long for the sisters to realize they had taken on more than a simple meals ministry which could be run out of a school cafeteria. And so, when the manager of a flophouse hotel in the city's skid row/historic district offered to turn over the hotel cafe grill to the sisters, they and the Springfield Catholic Parishes seized the opportunity.

They organized volunteers from six Catholic parishes to run the ministry, with a parish taking one day each week to cook and serve an evening meal and then clean up. Once again, it didn't take long for the sisters and the volunteers to see that providing evening meals was just the tip of the iceberg of needs. The hotel primarily housed people off the street. Many were mentally ill; many were elderly. Since Springfield had no homeless shelter, those who couldn't get into the hotel slept on the streets.

So, like many programs set up to feed the hungry, right from the start, the ministry developed into something more than providing just a hot meal. By 1985, the sisters had incorporated the ministry as The Kitchen, a not-for-profit freestanding corporation with a volunteer 21-member interdenominational board of trustees. Its mission is "rooted in the mission of Jesus and the healing ministry of the church and is dedicated to meeting needs of the displaced members." They leased the rundown hotel, and for 5 years, volunteers ran the growing number of programs.

Today, a full-time staff of 30 people allows The Kitchen to offer a continuum of care designed to rehabilitate, not recycle. State and federal grant money as well as more than 4,000 to 5,000 volunteer hours per month keep the ministries going.

The Kitchen's services have expanded to include four levels of housing: emergency transient shelter for one to two nights; stabilization housing in 18 apartments for singles and families for up to 18 months; permanent housing for the elderly; and permanent housing in the 90-unit single-room-occupancy Missouri Hotel. Other services include family nurturing and counseling and child care; substance abuse and psychiatric counseling; medical and dental clinics staffed by volunteer medical personnel who see more than 700 people per month; social service assistance; low-income retirement for the elderly poor; relocation services and aftercare; transportation aid; clothing and household assistance (e.g., budgeting, parenting, and communications); legal clinic; job counseling; and emergency financial assistance for food, rent, and utilities.

Education components include GED and literacy programs, survival skills (e.g., budgeting, parenting, and communications), tutoring, and nutritional instruction. A job skills training program has components in housekeeping services; manual labor skills such as furniture, upholstery, and small appliance repair; and culinary arts training. Fresh Start involves community leaders and organizations in providing financial counseling and survival skills so hotel residents can transition to their own apartments in the city.

In 1994, The Kitchen housed 2,175 people in the hotel; provided 85,100 days of shelter; helped 464 families through Fresh Start; provided free medical care to 7,201 people; and provided free dental care to 62 people.

And, The Kitchen continues to do what it first set out to do over a decade ago—feed the hungry. The Missouri Hotel serves cafeteria-style meals three times a day, 365 days a year, free to anyone who is hungry. In 1994, The Kitchen served 170,500 meals. In addition, volunteers assisted 3,116 households encompassing 8,623 people with emergency food. The Kitchen receives so much free food that their monthly food bill is less than $1,000, and each month they donate surplus food to two food pantries in rural Missouri.

Making a home for The Kitchen in the six-block historic district has at times been more difficult than feeding and sheltering the needy who live there, director Sister Lorraine Biebel admits. For example, in 1986 neighbors tried "to run us out of town," she says. But, good even came of that, she says, when Springfield's mayor created a task force on homelessness. The task force eventually challenged The Kitchen to increase their services.

In 1995, after news got out that The Kitchen had received a $1 million federal Housing and Urban Development grant to hire more professional staff and after local media stories accused The Kitchen of "serving freeloaders," Sister Lorraine learned she needed to "stay tuned to the outside as well as keeping our noses to the grindstone" of ministry. "Now, we are trying to stay in dialogue with our neighbors," she says.

Finding a Ministry Niche

The brightly colored domes of Harvard University dominate the skyline. The stately buildings of Massachusetts Institute of Technology (MIT) line the banks of the Charles River. Century-old homes stand side by side with quaint restaurants and storefronts. The sights and sounds of the world mingle in Harvard Square.

This is Cambridge, Massachusetts, just across the Charles River from Boston. It is a city which mirrors the paradoxes of American life. It is a city whose architecture and institutions stand as reminders of Cambridge's influence on the history of the nation and the world. It is a city whose world-class institutions of higher learning draw the world's brightest and best students who look to a bright tomorrow. It is a city of affluence and yet a city where more than 5,000 homeless cannot see beyond the needs of today.

In such a setting, it would be easy for a church to focus only on long-term Cambridge residents or only on students, but for Metropolitan Baptist Church, neither is an option. The 30-year-old Southern Baptist congregation with a Sunday morning attendance of 70 has chosen to minister to both these groups and to the needy as well. For the church, it is what being church is all about.

Knowing the parameters of a small membership and limited resources, Metropolitan did its homework before beginning a ministry to the needy in the mid-1980s. Not wanting to duplicate available services, then-pastor Tom McKibbens went to city leaders to ascertain what needs were not being met by other churches and community agencies. What he learned became Metropolitan's ministry niche: a community meal on Saturday, since no free meals were available in the city on weekends; a place to shower; and a place to do laundry.

Networking with other Southern Baptists led to money from a private foundation to remodel the church basement and to install showers and money from a church in Richmond, Virginia, to purchase a washer and dryer. Boston-area Southern Baptist churches were enlisted to help provide and serve the hot meals. Money to cover additional costs came from the Southern Baptist Convention's Hunger Relief Funds.

And so, for more than 10 years, each Saturday 150 of Cambridge's needy come to Metropolitan. Some have no home other than the street. Others are marginally homeless, living in temporary shelters. While most are unemployed, some work for wages which do not begin to cover the Boston area's high cost of living. Over the years, Metropolitan has seen the number of families who come increase dramatically.

They come to take a shower, to use the washer and dryer, and to choose clothes from the racks of clothes set up in the front of the sanctuary. They stay for the community meal and fellowship. Some return to worship on Sunday morning.

When Dale Cross succeeded Tom as pastor in 1991, he brought an important new dimension to Metropolitan's ministry. He joined in the formation of the Christian Economic Coalition (CEC) of Boston, an interdenominational coalition of business, legal, and religious leaders who want to create 150 businesses with 5,000 worker-owners over a 10-year period for the homeless and marginally employed of the inner city. The CEC is modeled on page 108. Through the CEC, they hope to address some of the root causes of hunger and homelessness in their city.

Metropolitan also works with other congregations in their section of Cambridge through the Porter Square Ecumenical Center. The center includes a dozen churches and three community organizations which seek to coordinate time, energies, and money in addressing the needs of Cambridge's poor. They are working to get the city of Cambridge to buy a house to be used as a day center for the homeless.

Christian Economic Coalition: Working for Change in Boston

"Imagine this scenario: Haitians, Latinos, African Americans, and Anglos cooperating along with Brazilians, Jamaicans, Koreans and Chinese to rebuild our cities. United by faith in Jesus Christ, Catholics, Pentecostals, evangelicals and mainline Protestants work together towards a new economic model, and a common goal: using business to build a whole new culture in their neighborhoods—a community of hope, faith, respect, and hard work."[13]

That is a description of a grassroots movement of inner-city churches in Boston, Massachusetts, which began in the early 1990s. The movement, under the auspices of the CEC of Boston, sponsors worker-owned cooperative businesses which are seeking to rebuild communities. They hope to create 150 new businesses and 5,000 jobs over a 10-year period.

The first class of 20 people hoped to begin 16 businesses. By early 1996, 9 businesses seemed likely to be successful, 3 had disappeared, and 4 others possibly may pull through. The strong ones include a day-care business, a beauty parlor, a barber shop, a construction company with ten employees, a company recycling building materials, a home health-care company, and a $2 million roller skating rink.[14]

Mark Heim, a professor at Andover Newton Theological Seminary in Newton Centre, Massachusetts, described the work of the CEC in an article in the July 5–12, 1995, *Christian Century:*[15]

God's Long Shot in the Inner City: A Vision of Church-Based Economic Development by S. Mark Heim

On an early spring evening almost a hundred people gather in the Dorchester Temple Baptist Church. One wall in the church's entryway is painted black and carries a long list of the names of teenagers and children whose lives have been taken by violence in the sections of Boston surrounding the church. The names on the wall do not come up at the meeting, though they are not far from anyone's mind. There is a good deal of prayer and scripture reading. But this is not a midweek worship service. It is a business meeting. The people here are part of a program whose goal is to create 150 new businesses and 5,000 jobs in the next ten years. It is a key step in an effort to transform the economic landscape of this inner city.

Fourteen business teams are starting a 15-week training program run by the Christian Economic Coalition of Boston. Almost all the teams are attempting to start new enterprises. A few are hoping to expand or secure existing ones. An urban church sponsors each team, and in some cases the pastor is a member of the team. Each team includes people who live in the neighborhoods that were home to the young people whose names appear on the wall: Roxbury, Dorchester, and Mattapan. And all of them are committed to something more than personal economic security. They hope to take part in the revitalization of their communities.

One team plans to open a cooperative restaurant. A group of construction workers intend to form a cooperative so that they can bid on jobs in the role of contractor rather than simply work as employees for someone else. A team representing an existing recycling company seeks a strategy to expand and employ more people. Six women street preachers have covenanted to start a day-care center. As each of the teams shares its visions, several themes are repeated: "We need to show our young people that education and hard work do pay off." "We want to employ the young men on our streets." "We want to make our neighborhoods attractive again." "We want to strengthen families by working with children and their parents."

The excitement this evening may be hard to justify. For all the dreams and dollars expended on it, inner-city economic development has run the gamut from ignominious failure to success of the most negligible sort. As the *New York Times* reported: "Conservatives love it. Liberals love it. Foundations love it. The churches love it. But of all things undertaken in the inner cities, the one most likely to fail is community economic development." Or as one longtime activist put it, "I've flushed more money down the toilet of economic development than I care to remember." Another explained: "We're good at community development. But for 20 years we have failed at entrepreneurial development. The most we seem able to do is market our neighborhoods to outside corporations." The goal of locally owned, locally managed and locally staffed businesses has remained a dream.

What is different about the Christian Economic Coalition? The answer can be found in part by turning from the inner city to international development. One of the most successful and innovative Christian-based international development agencies is Opportunity International. Opportunity adopted and refined a microloan philosophy, helping to establish partner agencies in more than 40 countries around the world whose modest loans have compiled an enviable record in both job creation and repayment of those loans.

For some time Opportunity has contemplated an even more daunting challenge: economic development for poor communities in the U.S. The organization's board members were well aware of the many failed attempts in this area, and they were also aware that they could not simply transfer their international model to the urban U.S. Something new was needed. A task force was established to seek the most promising existing model. Opportunity eventually settled on the work of the Christian Economic Coalition in Boston as having the most potential to transform the economics of the inner city.

Roger Dewey, CEC's executive director, has been developing his vision since 1968. In the wake of Martin Luther King Jr.'s assassination, Dewey felt God's call to address both society's racial divide and the needs of the city. CEC emphasizes church-based, self-help economic progress through cooperative ownership of local businesses. The coalition's leadership comes not only from residents of the inner city, but from the churches of the inner city. Many people from the suburbs—including bankers, lawyers, businesspeople and professors—participate in the coalition, but they function in the spirit of what an earlier CEC structure called a board of servants. Decision making lies in the hands of a board composed almost entirely of inner-city pastors and church members.

CEC is a rich mix of realism and vision. The board and staff include people who have had the experience of developing a business from scratch to multimillion-dollar status, and also people who have seen their enterprises go under more than once. They do not subscribe to the notion that everyone has what it takes to start a successful business or to handle key managerial roles. They recognize that nearly all new businesses (in any community) fail because of bad business plans, inadequate financial record-keeping, unrealistic projections, tax and legal problems, and insufficient credit or capital. In the inner city, these ordinary hurdles loom even higher, partly because of the lack of resources in the community and partly due to discrimination and suspicion on the part of established institutions.

CEC's realism is balanced by a vision. That vision stems first of all from scripture. CEC is convinced that rebuilding the city is God's aim and that the church is the network that has the means to accomplish this. The instrumental skeleton for the CEC vision comes from the Mondragon cooperatives of Spain. Founded by a priest in the Basque region of Spain after World War II, Mondragon is an economic miracle of sorts. This unique network of worker-owned cooperatives now comprises more than 200 distinct businesses, and has an extraordinary success rate in starting new businesses. The genius of Mondragon has been its multiplier effect. It did not simply succeed in starting many profitable businesses; it linked these businesses in mutually supportive relationships. For example, one of its businesses is a bank whose primary customers are other cooperatives. Another is a printing enterprise that serves other Mondragon members as well as ordinary customers. The success of one business strengthens the others. The network also is used to shift workers and managers from one firm to another when the need arises. Similarly, within each worker-owned business economic squeezes are met with collective strategies to prevent layoffs.

The Mondragon vision is reflected in CEC's organization, which has four operational arms. The first is the Training Institute, which provides intensive preparation in biblical principles, business basics and CEC's vision. It is the incubator for new businesses. The second is CEC's central office. The office is prepared to maintain financial records for businesses, especially in the early years. It can provide professional analysis, help generate financial reports, deal with tax requirements and government regulations, and cut costs by consolidation. The third arm is a consulting division in which CEC maintains a roster of experts (currently volunteers); CPAs, marketing experts, management advisers, lawyers, and people to do feasibility research. The fourth arm deals with capital resources. CEC is building its own revolving loan fund which will be used to finance some start-ups. A group of bankers and investment professionals works to assure venture capital from both the revolving fund and traditional sources.

CEC's goal is to have each of these four arms eventually spin off into businesses in their own rights, thriving on the success of the businesses they both empower and link with in the network. This is part of the comprehensive Mondragon vision; rather than watching the funds and resources go elsewhere, the community in which the new businesses arise share in the benefits of servicing those businesses.

CEC is unique on both ends of the business cycle. At the start-up phase, it brings in all the resources possible to see that the failings that often kill new businesses are anticipated and prevented. Yet it does not attempt to artificially suspend real-life economic dynamics. Instead, it provides what is necessary to overcome the built-in disadvantages for inner-city residents. At the phase of maturity, when businesses achieve some stability, CEC provides a structure to multiply that success in the surrounding community.

Will it work? CEC is in its own critical start-up phase. Opportunity International has invested $90,000 to help underwrite preparation of the first full-scale "class" of businesses. After 15 weeks of working with volunteer mentors to hammer out their plans, the teams will run their proposals by CEC's team of financial consultants. Once the plans pass this rigorous test, they go to CEC's board for approval and then to the investment committee before being authorized for CEC loan funds or recommended to area banks and investors.

Several businesses have already gone through CEC's pilot version of this process. The Chez Vous roller skating rink was for several years one of the vibrant youth centers in Boston. The couple who ran it provided a youth ministry in association with a local pastor. When other owners took it over, the rink became known instead for a series of confrontations and shootings. The original owners have worked through the CEC process to develop a business plan for a new skating rink and youth ministry, and are attracting venture capital with coalition support.

A woman who runs her own one-person cleaning business went through CEC's training process. Under the direction of CEC's volunteers she developed a business plan, became legally incorporated as Sunshine Home Services and conducted a survey of the market that allowed her to restructure her prices. The result was greater stability and the addition of three employees. Sunshine Home Services was also the first business to have all its financial records computerized in the central CEC office. The founder has committed to contributing a tithe of the business's profits to CEC each year.

In another case, the founder of an 11-year-old home health care service was on the verge of retirement. She considered buy-out plans, but hoped to preserve employment for her 80 workers and maintain the service commitment of her business. CEC is helping the employees understand how they can buy the company themselves, through an Employee Stock Ownership Program conversion. Many of them are fearful, as they have never imagined themselves in charge. Four MBA students from Harvard University are researching the market to see how to develop the company for maximum security and growth potential. Meanwhile, CEC is working with the employees to develop the confidence and knowledge necessary for them to take this step.

The current crop of business teams has ambitious plans. The odds are still daunting. But very few new businesses (except those spun off from corporate giants) have such an extensive support system of group training and idea sharing. Above all, the business teams have a strong church connection. A whole network of people is invested personally and even financially in their success. They are upheld in prayer, but also held accountable by other parishioners.

It is frequently observed that churches are often the most viable local institutions in inner-city neighborhoods. But attempts to root economic development in the churches have had sporadic success at best. The Mondragon model has spawned intense interest among economists and activists over the past decades, but it has never been duplicated on its original scale. The Catholicism and the distinctive Basque cultural cohesion of the Mondragon participants appear to be key factors in their success. At a recent conference on Mondragon-type development, a longtime secular enthusiast acknowledged that an unusual dimension of commitment seems to be required to maintain worker-owned cooperatives or mutual support among businesses. If Mondragon-type development were ever to come about in the U.S., he said, it would probably have to be based in churches where people would "do it for God, or something."

At Dorchester Temple the evening training session is almost over. Trainers emphasize that teams will not be financed (whether by CEC or by banks that already look upon the inner city as a lost cause) because they have good motives or an impressive dream. "You have to be able to show what your resources are, what the obstacles are, what your plan is and why it is going to work. Before we are finished you are going to be able to do that backward and forward."

That said, team members shuffle their business textbooks under their Bibles and gather for several minutes of fervent prayer. This primary resource won't appear on the executive summaries for a bank loan officer; those business proposals will stand on their own. But the people behind them don't. . . .

The scripture text CEC refers to continually comes from the Book of Nehemiah. It is the passage about Nehemiah and the people of Israel returning from exile to rebuild the walls of a devastated Jerusalem. Each family restores the portion of the wall in their immediate neighborhood, but as they work together in the common task the result is a whole new city. CEC expresses a similar calling: to replace the wall of lamentation with a new wall of economic protection for the community. There have been a lot of false starts in rebuilding Jerusalem, but it still seems like the ideal construction project: challenging and rewarding work with unmatched long-term job security.

Put Your Faith to Work

(Ideas require minimal time involvement and may serve as entry points for a hunger ministry or as onetime ministry projects.)

Give. Contribute money or food. If you have little to give, put your creativity to work to raise money or get involved in existing money-raising efforts such as the Church World Services CROP Walk. In 1992, 322,000 people participated in CROP walk.

Begin a food pantry in your church or local group of churches. Stock it with nonperishable items such as peanut butter, flour, dry beans, rice, oatmeal, and pasta.

Glean. Gather surplus food—from the harvest fields to day-old goods in the grocery—to distribute to the needy. "Rescue" excess, unsold food from restaurants, hotels, catering companies, and other food service establishments and then distribute it to nonprofit agencies which serve meals to needy people.

Organize a food drive to stock church food pantries. Consult the pantry director about what things are needed.

Serve. Prepare and deliver food to the needy, the elderly, and the handicapped through such programs as Meals on Wheels and soup kitchens.

Volunteer at a food pantry as a receptionist, bagger, greeter, or food sorter.

Advocate. Get involved in hunger advocacy groups which seek to support public policies that can address both the symptoms and root causes of hunger and impoverishment. Support includes such things as writing letters and making phone calls to governmental personnel, getting medical coverage, and visiting members of Congress about specific legislation that affects the poor and hungry. (See p. 21 for guidelines on being an effective advocate.)

Selected Resources for Hunger Ministry

The following resources offer specific, detailed help on how to get started in hunger ministry.

Books

Butler, Cathy. *Servants of the Banquet.* Birmingham, AL: New Hope, 1993. Stories from around the nation and the world about Christians who are making a difference in combating hunger. Many ministry ideas are included at the end of each chapter.

Sider, Ronald. *Cry Justice: The Bible on Hunger and Poverty.* Downers Grove, IL: InterVarsity Press, 1980. A look at biblical texts on poverty, possessions, justice, and stewardship.

Sider, Ronald. *Rich Christians in an Age of Hunger.* Downers Grove, IL: InterVarsity Press, 1977. Gives a biblical perspective on hunger, property, and wealth. Suggests practical things individual Christians and churches can do to live more simply as well as be more proactive in addressing the needs of the hungry.

Periodicals

Seeds, P. O. Box 6170, Waco, TX 76706. Subscription price: $20 for 1 year; $38 for 2 years. Biblically based magazine with articles and ideas on grassroots efforts to fight hunger.

Video

One Common Need. Birmingham, AL: New Hope, 1996. Explores the scope of hunger, its effects, its cause, and some solutions that are working. To order call 1 (800) 968-7301.

Pamphlets

From Home Mission Board, 4200 North Point Parkway, Alpharetta, GA 30202:
Church and Community Needs Survey Guide

Beginning a Food Distribution Ministry
How Your Church Can Minister with Homeless People
Domestic Hunger

Advocacy Groups

Bread for the World, 1100 Wayne Avenue, Suite 1000, Silver Spring, MD 20910; (301) 608-2400. Bread for the World does not directly distribute food or relief; it monitors legislation pertaining to hunger issues and alerts people to ways they can affect public policy relating to the poor and hungry.

Food Banks

Second Harvest, 116 South Michigan Avenue, Suite 4, Chicago, IL 60603-6001; (312) 263-2303. Second Harvest is a network of 185 affiliated food banks in the United States which provide food to the hungry through nearly 50,000 social service agencies. Annually, it distributes more than 500 million pounds of surplus food and grocery products to its food banks. The food banks in turn channel the food to local nonprofit charities.

Seven Priority Areas for Transformative Action Against Hunger

- Individuals and agencies assisting hungry people can expand what they do to influence government policies.
- Religious communities can teach how social concern flows from a relationship with God and help motivate involvement in effective political action.
- Low-income people's organizations can be strengthened, especially in their capacity to influence government policies that affect them.
- Organizations which help low-income people can more fully engage people of color, especially in decision making.
- The media can move beyond stories of pity and charity to explain the causes of hunger, and people and organizations concerned about hunger can make a bigger effort to influence the media.

•People can expand and strengthen antihunger advocacy organizations.

•People and organizations working against poverty and hunger can become more aware of themselves as part of a large, potentially dynamic movement.

Source: Bread for the World, *Hunger 1994: Transforming the Politics of Hunger,* as repeated in *Hunger 1995: Causes of Hunger,* 29.

What the Bible Says About Hunger and Poverty
Proverbs 19:17; 21:13; Matthew 25:31–46; Luke 14:12–14

Notes

[1] Donald A. Atkinson and Charles L. Roesel, *Meeting Needs, Sharing Christ* (Nashville: LifeWay Press, 1995), 27–28.

[2] David Beckmann, "Introduction," *Hunger 1994: Transforming the Politics of Hunger* (Silver Spring, MD: Bread for the World Institute, 1993), 1.

[3] Richard A. Hoehn, "Feeding People—Half of Overcoming Hunger," *Hunger 1994: Transforming the Politics of Hunger,* 12.

[4] Beckmann, "Introduction," 1.

[5] Ibid.

[6] "Child Poverty in U.S. Reaches Highest Level in 30 Years," *Western Recorder,* April 4, 1995, 1.

[7] "How Hungry Is America?" *Newsweek,* March 14, 1994, 58.

[8] Ibid., 59.

[9] Ibid., 58.

[10] Beckmann, "Introduction," 2.

[11] Ibid., 6–7.

[12] Richard A. Hoehn, "Religious Communities Respond to Hunger," *Hunger 1994: Transforming the Politics of Hunger* (Silver Spring, MD: Bread for the World Institute, 1993), 32.

[13] Roger Dewey, "Nehemiah Would Be Proud," *Prism,* November-December 1995, 22.

[14] Ibid.

[15] S. Mark Heim, "God's Long Shot in the Inner City: A Vision of Church-Based Economic Development," *Christian Century,* July 5–12, 1995, 680–82.

"My mother belongs to a church in Collinsville, Illinois, that had a fine substitute teacher at its Lutheran school. Unknown to the teacher's family, she had been visiting a gambling boat. Money the family thought had gone to pay the rent and family bills had, instead, gone into wagers. One day, she left a message for her family, drove her car to a shopping center, and killed herself."

—Senator Paul Simon

"The church needs to focus on the waste and wreckage of human life that is a consequence of gambling. Gambling is a pastime that can turn into a profound addiction or pathological gambling."

—Wayne Oates

"Each day, a young businessman in Gulfport, Mississippi, left his office fully intending to take the day's receipts to the bank. Instead, each day he stopped at a casino to gamble. Now, he's working to overcome his addiction. Each day, he turns the receipts over to his wife for her to make the bank deposit."

—John Landrum, Baptist chaplain, Gulfport, Mississippi

6

$\mathcal{U}$nmasking Gambling

To gamble and win big seems to be the new American dream. Not only have individual Americans got caught up in gambling's grasp, but local governments, state governments, and Native American Indian tribes have latched onto gambling as a quick source of income for their cash-strapped entities. During the past 15 years, lotteries, riverboat casinos, video poker, and charitable bingo have sprung up across the country to entice Americans to try their luck at something for nothing.

Today, legalized gambling is the fastest growing industry in the United States.[1] It is an industry that had net revenues of $29.9 billion in 1992—that's the amount of money gamblers lost. (The total amount wagered that year was $329 billion.)[2] By 1994, the amount wagered legally reached $482 billion—a 15 percent jump from the year before.[3] By the end of 1995, the figure was more than $500 billion.[4] That was a far cry from the $17 billion legally wagered in 1974.[5]

In 1995, lotteries accounted for $13 billion in income. Indian gaming took in $2 billion. Greater Atlantic City casinos took in more than $77 billion, and Nevada casinos took in more than $180 billion.[6]

During the 6 years from 1988 to 1994, total yearly casino revenues rose from $8 billion to about $15 billion.[7]

According to casino industry sources, between 1990 and 1993, the number of American households in which at least one person visited a casino doubled, from 46 million to 92 million. More than three-fourths of the increase came from people visiting casinos outside Nevada and Atlantic City.[8]

Gambling: Historical Nuggets

While the last 15 years have seen a marked increase in legalized gambling in the United States, gambling is not a new development. In a report to the United States Senate on July 31, 1995, Illinois senator Paul Simon traced its history:

"The Bible and early historical records tell of its existence. Gambling surfaced early in US history, then largely disappeared as a legal form of revenue for state and local governments. It remained very much alive, however, even though illegal, in the back rooms of taverns and in not-so-hidden halls, often with payoffs to public officials to 'look the other way' while it continued. . . . "Early in our nation's history, almost all states had some form of lottery, my state of Illinois was no exception. When Abraham Lincoln served in our state legislature from 1834 to 1842, lotteries were authorized, and there apparently was no moral question raised about having them. . . .

"In Illinois and other states the loose money quickly led to corruption, and the states banned all forms of gambling. Illinois leaders felt so strongly about it, they put the ban into the state constitution. For many years, Louisiana had the only lottery, and then in 1893—after a major scandal there—the federal government prohibited all lottery sales. Even the results of tolerated but illegal lotteries could not be sent through the mail.

"But the lottery crept back in, first in New Hampshire in 1963, and then in 36 other states."[9]

Until the 1960s, legalized gambling was confined to Nevada. Even as recently as 1988, only Nevada and New Jersey offered casino gambling.[10] But since that time legalized gambling has spread to an additional 47 states so that now, only Hawaii and Utah have no form of legalized gambling.[11]

Gambling venues have expanded from Las Vegas slot machines and blackjack tables to casinos on Indian reservations and riverboats. Legalized gambling now also includes on- and offtrack betting, state-run lotteries, bingo, video poker, blackjack, craps, baccarat, roulette, and sports wagering. And, in some cities, it is possible to bet on horse racing in the privacy of your living room through an interactive home-betting system.[12]

In addition, horse and dog racing are now legal in almost every state. And in Wisconsin, wagering on snowmobile races is too.[13] There even are reports of plans for back-of-seat slot machines on some airline flights.[14]

In 1985, Montana became the first state to legalize slot machines in bars. Four years later, South Dakota authorized its state lottery agency to use a version of slot machines (called video lottery terminals, or VLTs) in bars and convenience stores. Oregon, Rhode Island, West Virginia, and Louisiana soon followed suit. By 1991, Oregon had also legalized betting on sports teams and electronic keno machines through its state lottery.[15] In fact, electronic gambling machines are the fastest-growing sector of the industry.[16]

Between 1988 and 1994, 23 states legalized commercial gambling casinos;[17] and 10 states legalized video slot or poker machines at racetracks and bars.

The turning point in government-sponsored gambling came in 1991 when Iowa became the first state to legalize casino gambling on riverboats. Illinois, Mississippi, and Louisiana soon followed suit.[18]

Statistics are staggering. By August 1995:

•Twenty-four states had commercial or Indian casino gambling.

•Six states had approved floating casinos. Mississippi, alone, had 27 boats.

•One hundred twenty-five million people had visited casinos during the previous year.[19]

•Thirty-nine states had lotteries.

•One hundred fifteen Indian tribes had some form of casino gambling.[20]

•Three-fourths of the nation's citizens lived within 300 miles of a casino.[21]

Gambling: The Lure of Legality

Today, many local governments view casinos and lotteries as a cure for their economic troubles and the gambling industry is more than ready to bill itself as "beneficent saviors," says Robert Goodman, in his landmark book, *The Luck Business.*[22]

Thus, the explosive growth of casinos in the early 1990s came on the backs of economically declining communities, such as rural Mississippi and older industrial cities in Iowa, Illinois, Indiana, and Louisiana.[23]

Through masterful public relations campaigns, promoters of legalized gambling point to the new revenue and/or new jobs it brings to a community. And it does seem to work—temporarily. Senator Simon writes: "While the promises of what legalized gambling will do for a community or state almost always are greatly exaggerated, it is also true that many communities who are desperate for revenue and feel they have no alternative are helped."[24]

Simon cites the cities of East St. Louis, Illinois, and Bridgeport, Connecticut, as examples of cities that find themselves with enough revenue to at least take care of minimal services after legalizing gambling.[25]

And, in the case of legalized gambling on Indian reservations, Simon says that with "misery as their constant companion" in the form of high unemployment rates, alcoholism rates, suicide rates, and poverty indexes, "it should not surprise anyone that tribal leaders who want to produce for their people seize what some view as a legal loophole that our courts and laws have created to get revenue for their citizens." Native American leaders who see long-term harm to their tribes from the gambling enterprises are hard-pressed by those who see immediate benefits, and not too much hope for sizable revenue outside of gambling."[26]

Senator Simon is quick to point out that in most cases, the love affair with legalized gambling is short-lived as problems quickly surface.

In reality, gambling is a multifaceted problem with tentacles which reach deep into American society to touch not only society through rising crime rates, economics and politics but also the individual and the family unit.

Gambling and Crime

The gambling industry likes to sweep crime problems attendant to gambling venues under the rug. In Chicago, for example, when officials wanted to bring in a $2 billion casino which they said would create 10,000 construction jobs, a report by the Chicago Crime Commission that "organized crime will infiltrate casino operations and unions, and will be involved in related loan-sharking, prostitution, drug activities . . . and public corruption" went "almost unnoticed," Senator Simon reported.[27]

Instead, the *Chicago Sun-Times* noted, "The sooner state law changes to allow land-based casino gambling, the better. And the sooner Chicago finally gets in on the action, the better."[28]

In Atlantic City, in just 3 years following the opening of its first casino, the number of crimes nearly tripled. In 1983, one report stated that "street crime has run rampant, and prostitution has become so widespread that the city's chief of police, in despair of curbing it, recommended that it be legalized." In addition, crime spilled over into many nearby communities as well.[29]

And across the nation, it is estimated that 40 percent of all white-collar crime has its roots in gambling.[30]

Gambling and Economics

Legalized gambling is bad for local businesses, is good for bankruptcy courts, and produces no new wealth or jobs, according to University of Illinois professor John Kindt. "Legalized gambling is a regressive tax on the poor. It makes poor people poorer. And it intensifies every social problem that exists," he says.[31]

A case in point is Deadwood, South Dakota, a small community that was the first place outside Nevada and Atlantic City to legalize casino gambling. When the state legalized limited-stakes casino gambling in 1989,[32] the town was promised "economic development, new jobs, and lower taxes," according to the county's prosecuting attorney. However, the casinos flourished, but other businesses did not. Testifying before a US House committee in September 1994, Jeffrey Bloomberg said that businesses which "provide the necessities of life such as clothing are no longer available . . . and customers of the town's only remaining grocery store walk a gauntlet of slot machines as they exit with their purchases. . . . For the most part, the jobs which were created earn minimum wage or slightly better and are without benefits. . . . As for the claim that gambling brings tax relief, this simply has not proven true. Real property taxes for both residential and commercial properties have risen each and every year since gambling was legalized. . . . Crimes of theft embezzlement, bad checks and other forms of larceny [have increased]"[33]

In fact, some industry insiders now are admitting that because most gambling in the future will be done locally and will not tap the tourist market, it may not be the boon to local economies some states believed it would be when they rushed to legalize it.[34]

And, early promises of revenue from state-run lotteries often are revised downward as time passes, thus opening the door for other gambling venues to be legalized.

A few years after Kentucky passed the state lottery, the Louisville *Courier-Journal,* ran a story saying, "As a provider of revenue for the state, Kentucky's lottery—at least as it exists now—has probably peaked. The state is not likely to get much more revenue than it is getting now from the lottery."[35]

The January 1996 article cited "gambling competition in the region, especially from Indiana riverboat casinos," as the reason for reduced revenue and raised the question, "So, should Kentucky's lottery consider offering other forms of gambling—including such casino-like games as video poker and keno [called active gaming], which could put another $100 million or more into the state's general fund?" Overall lottery ticket sales in Kentucky for the 1995 fiscal year totalled $513 million, with $142 million returned to the state.[36]

Rather than raising tax revenues, gambling costs the private sector $2.75 to $4.75 for every dollar the government collects in taxes, according to University of Illinois professor Earl Grinols. "It's incomprehensible that a state would choose gambling to raise tax revenue," Grinols says, "but the problem is most states do not know these numbers."[37]

And, from a purely economic standpoint, a substantial case can be made against gambling, according to Paul Samuelson, the distinguished Nobel Prize-winning economist. "It involves simply sterile transfers of money or goods between individuals, creating no new money or goods. Although it creates no output, gambling does nevertheless absorb time and resources. When pursued beyond the limits of recreation . . . gambling subtracts from the national income."[38]

Gambling and Politics

Gambling is changing the role of government from regulation to the point of preying on citizens by enticing them to gamble so states can collect more revenue, according to Goodman. "The proliferation of legalized gambling in America is probably the only example of a situation where government is not simply legalizing a potentially harmful activity, but is actually promoting it," he says.[39]

Goodman contends that through advertising, media promotions, and public relations campaigns, the government explicitly tries to get people to gamble more. He makes a strong case that the government preys on people's hopes for a better life, manipulates their psychological needs, and preys on their adversity.

He contends that the growth of gambling "has taken place against a backdrop where, for more and more Americans, working for a living is no longer seen as a potential path to a better life." During the 1980s and early 1990s, he says, "People in all walks of life were offered new opportunities for financial risk taking. Gambling was just one of a myriad of techniques for making money through luck rather than work, which included new strategies for speculating in real estate, the stock market, and collectibles."[40]

Gambling and Social Problems

Gambling "intensifies every social problem that exists," Kindt says. When gambling is first introduced, "there are some benefits," he says. "But when compared with the costs, this is not a close call."[41]

Jeffrey Bloomberg, prosecuting attorney in the rural town of Deadwood, South Dakota, graphically describes the impact of gambling. Within 5 years after the town became the only non-Indian community allowed to have casino gambling, Deadwood, with a population of 1,800 people, had 82 casinos.

"We have seen individuals who, prior to their exposure to gambling, had no criminal history, who were not junkies or alcoholics, many of whom had good jobs, who became hooked on slot machines and after losing all their assets and running all credit resources to their maximum began committing some type of crime to support their addiction," Bloomberg says.[42]

"Our office has also seen an increase in the number of child abuse and neglect cases as a result of gambling. These run the spectrum from the children left in their cars all night while their parents gamble, to the children left at home alone while their parents gamble, to the children left at home alone while single mothers work the casino late shift, to the household without utilities or groceries because one or both parents have blown their paycheck gambling."[43]

The suicide rates for problem gamblers is significantly higher than for the general population, according to Senator Simon. One out of five attempt suicide.[44]

John Landrum, a Baptist chaplain to the casinos in Gulfport, Mississippi, has seen those problems firsthand. He says that within a year and a half after Mississippi legalized casino gambling in 1992, the social problems had "directly or indirectly affected every person in the state."[45]

In his 3 years of ministry, Landrum has seen many people lose their homes and businesses and many lose their marriages as gambling has worked its way into their lives. And many of those people were local Mississippians.

It is gambling's daily lure to local residents which concerns William Thompson, a professor of public administration at the University of Nevada, Las Vegas.

"It's bad to have casinos available to people on a day-to-day basis," he says. "There are casinos off 'the Strip' in Vegas that cater to the local residents, and that does absolutely no good for our community. By making gamblers out of people who live here, we're going to wind up in pretty sad shape. . . . I think urban areas that welcome in casinos will begin to feel some of those problems."

Moreover, he says, "Businesses stay away from here [Las Vegas] because they don't want their employees gambling. I don't think other communities will want that, either."[46]

A high official in Nevada state government concurred. He told Senator Simon, "If we could get rid of gambling in our state, it would be the best thing that could happen to us. I cannot say that publicly for political reasons. But major corporations that might locate their principle offices here or build plants here don't do it. They know that gambling brings with it serious personnel problems."[47]

Gambling and Morality

The very clear trend in the United States and the world is that more and more people accept gambling as morally and ethically OK, according to those who study gambling trends. Thus, the moral argument doesn't often pay off. Even the term *gambling* is seldom used in the industry, giving way to the more pleasing term *gaming*.

Gambling and the Christian

Increasingly, as legalized gambling has gone local, Christians have gotten entangled in its web.

With today's easy access to all sorts of gambling venues, Christians who once would have been adamantly opposed to gambling in any form can easily move from tolerance to acceptance to use. Even in the Bible Belt, gambling has caught on like wildfire—a phenomenon which has baffled sociologists and theologians alike. The fact that riverboat casinos and floating barges especially have been successful in the South has left industry watchers scratching their heads.

As betting opportunities have become more accessible, many Christians have rationalized their concerns. They too have bought into the false hope and false sense of security gambling promises.

It has become all too easy for Christians to fall for the line that gambling is a voluntary, victimless tax or a harmless entertainment. Issues of deception, the desire for money without working for it, the parasitism of gambling, and the threat of an addictive behavior are being forgotten.

"Most of the gambling addicts we deal with [in Gulf-port, Miss.] are Christians," Landrum says. "And we didn't expect that."

Gambling: The Deeper Roots

In his book *Luck: A Secular Faith,* pastoral psychologist Wayne Oates calls for a look at the deeper roots of gambling. Gambling, he says, is a part of the "horizontal religion" of luck: that is, a secular belief that omits the vertical belief in God as known in Jesus Christ."[48] He writes that a composite of the characteristics of a compulsive gambler "is the stuff of which the devotee of luck as a secular faith is made." Those characteristics are a subjective certainty that the gambler will win; he or she "just knows"; an unbounded faith in his or her own cleverness; and the claim that life is nothing but a gamble.[49]

Oates names three types of gambler: the fun-loving gambler who may bet on an event like the Kentucky Derby once a year, the professional gambler who makes a living at gambling, and the compulsive, pathological gambler who "is driven by an irrational set of unconscious forces" and whose view of the world and of himself or herself is severely distorted.[50] There are approximately 9 million adults and 1.3 million teenagers with some form of gambling addiction.[51]

Who gambles? Goodman writes: "The available nongambling industry research shows that a person's economic status tends to determine the psychological and financial meaning of gambling for that person—the higher one's income, the more one will tend to see gambling as entertainment or as a way to socialize with other people. Conversely, the lower one's income, the more gambling tends to be seen as a form of investment. For the poor, who have few alternative ways to invest—in real estate, the stock market, or elsewhere—gambling is seen less as play and more as a serious chance to transform their lives.

"The available evidence also demonstrates that while lower-income people do not, in absolute amounts, spend more than middle-income people on gambling, they do spend quite a bit more as a percentage of their income. This means that the poor are paying a much heavier tax only on the willing than are higher-income people. While no one is literally forcing the poor to gamble, the fact that they see gambling as one of their few opportunities for investment and transforming their lives—a point of view which governments and the gambling industry often highlight in their promotional campaigns—means their voluntary willingness to gamble represents what might be called the coercion of circumstance, certainly more so than it does for higher-income people.[52]

Is Gambling Losing Ground?

In the early 1990s, it looked like there was no limit to the expansionist mood of the gambling industry. But by late 1994, the mood had been somewhat tempered. At the polls, the industry found that public opinion was not with them. That year, there were ballot proposals for new casino expansion in at least 7 states. All failed, although some measures which called for adding new games in places where gambling already existed, or for retaining gambling, were approved, according to Goodman.[53]

For the first time in the war against gambling, opposing forces were sufficiently organized to get their message across. Political, social, and religious groups now were making their voices heard.

"I am encouraged in the fight against gambling," Tom Grey of the National Coalition Against Legalized Gambling, said in May 1995. Grey, a United Methodist minister, formed the organization in 1994 in Chicago.

"We have been beating them [the gambling industry] with the sacrifice and the willingness of people to stand up. And we've been beating them with the truth. If you have the truth, you don't have to have money and muscle. People power and truth is all it takes," he said.[54]

And, in January 1996, the National Coalition Against Legalized Gambling joined forces with the National Council of Churches and the Christian Coalition to work together to try to stop the spread of legal gambling in the United States. That month, the three opened a new Washington office to be headed by Grey, who said the interfaith venture was a signal that the nation's religious community is ready to take the offensive against the gambling industry.

Grey said the new group plans to establish a national commission to investigate legalized gambling's impact on cities, its alleged ties to organized crime, and the political influence the gambling industry wields through campaign contributions.[55]

Put Your Faith to Work

A Christian Response to Gambling

"First and foremost, settle the issue with yourself," Bill Miller, chaplain at Louisville's Churchill Downs, says. "Then develop your own safeguards against being sucked in."[56]

Pastoral counselor Wayne Oates agrees. "We decide in the inner depths of our being whether to trust God to provide for us or to play the odds, the changes, and the probabilities, and thus to gamble," he writes. "In both instances, the odds, the chances, and the probabilities are there. In the presence of God, they are temporal, creaturely realities. In a secular faith, they are imagined to be infinite, yet in our control."[57]

Study the Scriptures concerning the stewardship of possessions. Include in your study not only gambling but the more subtle issue of using one's income for frivolous or greedy purchases and selfish desires.

"To me, gambling is gambling, whether you're talking about horse racing, bingo, casino gambling, or taking a chance on a turkey," says Claude Witt, director of the Temperance League of Kentucky. "It causes human desperation. It victimizes the poor. It contradicts social responsibility. It produces the wrong attitudes toward work. It's a sophisticated form of stealing."

Oates writes, "When we consider such issues as weighing the odds, taking chances, considering probabilities, we are often involved in what the Bible calls temptation—or testing—as the crucible in which our character is formed. When we lift the innermost parts of our decision making to God in Jesus Christ by asking for the guidance of the Holy Spirit, we have the assurance offered by Paul in Romans 8:26-27: 'Likewise the Spirit helps us in our weakness; for we do not know how to pray as we ought, but that very Spirit intercedes with sighs too deep for words. And God, who searches the heart, knows what is the mind of the Spirit, because the Spirit intercedes for the saints according to the will of God.'"[58]

If you want to minister to people with a gambling problem, . . .

•Write a letter stating your stance on the proliferation of gambling to the editor of your local newspaper.

•Provide resources for your church media center on gambling.

•Plan community workshops that include a Christian perspective on gambling.

•Invite the youth of your church and community to dialogue with your group about the pitfalls of gambling. Include a strong biblical base for the use of possessions in the dialogue.

"The church needs to focus on the waste and wreckage of human life that is a consequence of gambling," Oates says. "Gambling is a pastime that can turn into a profound addiction or pathological gambling."[59]

•Find out if a Gambler's Anonymous or Gam-anon group meets in your community. Offer to help.

Why the Church Should Oppose Gambling

•The deception involved serves to remind us of Satan as the "father of lies." (See John 8:39–47.)

•The desire for money without working is an important part of the appeal of gambling.

•The parasitism of gambling, especially on the working poor, must be addressed.

•The threat of addiction is inherent in gambling, just as it is in the use of alcohol and other addictive drugs.

Source: Wayne Oates, *Luck: A Secular Faith* (Louisville: Westminster John Knox Press, 1995), 87.

Profile of a Compulsive Gambler

A person who exhibits at least five of the following behaviors may be a pathological, or compulsive, gambler according to the American Psychiatric Association.

•Preoccupation with gambling (e.g., fixated on past gambling experiences, handicapping or planning the next venture, or thinking of ways to finance gambling ventures).

•The need to "raise the stakes" (gamble with more money) in order to achieve the desired excitement.

•Repeated failures to control, limit, or stop gambling. Restlessness or irritability when attempting to taper off or stop gambling.

•Gambles as an escape from problems or a negative mood (e.g., feelings of helplessness, guilt, anxiety, depression).

•After losing money gambling, often returns another day to recoup funds ("chasing" one's losses).

•Lies to significant others to hide the extent of gambling.

•Engages in crimes such as forgery, fraud, theft, or embezzlement to pay for gambling.

•Has risked or lost an important relationship, job, or opportunity because of gambling.

•Borrows from others to provide money to relieve a desperate financial situation caused by gambling.

Source: *Diagnostic and Statistical Manual of Mental Disorders of the American Psychiatric Association,* as quoted in *Congressional Quarterly Researcher,* March 18, 1994, 248.

Biblical Insights on Gambling and God's Providence

John 8:39–47   Proverbs 3:5–10; 10:16; 17:16
Psalm 145:13–16   Ecclesiastes 7:12

Gambling: A Chronology

1800s
Gambling booms on the frontier, but public opinion increasingly grows against it:

•1832—Massachusetts and Pennsylvania become the first states to outlaw lottery games.

•July 6, 1835—Vigilantes lynch five gamblers in Natchez, Mississippi, a Mississippi River town where gambling had taken hold.

•August 2, 1876—Wild Bill Hickok, the legendary Indian scout and gambler, is shot dead while playing poker in Deadwood, South Dakota.

•1895—The Federal Lottery Act limits the distribution of lottery materials across state lines.

1930s
Nationwide economic distress spurs a revival of legalized gambling in several states:

•1931—To build tourism during the depression, Nevada legalizes most forms of gambling. Massachusetts decriminalizes bingo to help churches and charitable organizations raise money.

•1933—Michigan, New Hampshire, and Ohio legalize parimutuel betting.

1960s–1970s
Searching for additional revenue sources, states look to lotteries and other forms of gambling as forms of "voluntary taxation":

•1964—New Hampshire becomes the first state this century to sponsor a lottery, modeled on the Irish Sweepstakes.

•1978—New Jersey becomes the second state to legalize casino gambling and restricts it to a single location—the rundown resort community of Atlantic City.

1980s

Indian tribes win the right to operate gaming facilities on their reservations:

•February 25, 1987—US Supreme Court's ruling in *California v. Cabazon Band of Mission Indians* paves the way for Indian tribes to set up gambling operations if gambling is legal elsewhere in the state.

•1988—President Ronald Reagan signs the Indian Gaming Regulatory Act (IGRA), which establishes regulations for three classes of gambling.

•1989—South Dakota legalizes limited-stakes casino gambling in the historic mining town of Deadwood.

1990s

The gambling craze continues to grow in the US although limits are placed on betting on team sports:

•1990—On the heels of the Deadwood decision, Colorado voters approve casino-type gambling for three former mining towns.

•1991—Riverboat gambling returns to the stretch of the Mississippi adjoining Iowa.

•November 22, 1991—In a demonstration project, Massachusetts allows residents to play the state's lottery by telephone.

•October 28, 1992—President George Bush signs legislation barring lotteries involving bets on team sports; however, the four states that permit such wagering are exempted.

•1992—Louisiana narrowly approves legislation to establish a riverfront facility in New Orleans, becoming the third state to legalize casino gambling. Legal wagering in the US reaches a record $329.9 billion.

•November 22, 1993—Attorney generals from five New England states and New York issue a joint statement opposing the spread of legalized gambling. They warn that "increased gambling will lead to increased crime."

Source: *Congressional Quarterly Researcher,* March 18, 1994, 51.

Notes

[1] Dennis Camire and Keith White, "Gambling Industry Wary of Commission Idea," *Louisville (Ky.) Courier-Journal,* August 20, 1995, A8.

[2] Paul Simon, "The Explosive Growth of Gambling in the US," Report to the Senate, US Senate Floor, July 31, 1995, as reprinted in *Christian Ethics Today,* December 1995, 10.

[3] Camire and White, "Gambling Industry Wary," A8.

[4] Simon, "The Explosive Growth of Gambling," 10.

[5] Ibid.

[6] Tommy Starkes, "Developing Ministries to Gaming Communities," *Break-Out Modules* (Atlanta: Home Mission Board, n.d.), 2.

[7] Robert Goodman, *The Luck Business: The Devastating Consequences and Broken Promises of America's Gambling Explosion* (New York: Free Press, 1995), 2.

[8] Ibid., 3.

[9] Simon, "The Explosive Growth of Gambling," 10.

[10] Goodman, *The Luck Business,* 2.

[11] Camire and White, "Gambling Industry Wary," A8.

[12] Kirsten Haukebo, "Churchill Downs, Partners Test Interactive Home-Betting System," *Louisville (Ky.) Courier-Journal,* August 25, 1995.

[13] Starkes, *Developing Ministries to Gaming Communities,* 2.

[14] Simon, "The Explosive Growth of Gambling," 10.

[15] Goodman, *The Luck Business,* 5.

[16] Camire, "Gambling Industry Wary," A8.

[17] Goodman, *The Luck Business,* 2.

[18] Ibid., 5.

[19] Camire, "Gambling Industry Wary," A8.

[20] Simon, "The Explosive Growth of Gambling," 12.

[21] Ibid., 10.

[22] Goodman, *The Luck Business,* 63.

[23] Ibid., 26.

[24] Simon, "The Explosive Growth of Gambling," 11.

[25] Ibid.

[26] Ibid., 12.

[27] Ibid., 11.

[28] Ibid.

[29] Goodman, *The Luck Business,* 23.

[30] Simon, "The Explosive Growth of Gambling," 13.

[31]"Gambling Losing Ground, Opponent Says," *Louisville: (Ky.) Western Recorder,* May 30, 1995, 7.

[32]*Congressional Quarterly Researcher,* March 18, 1994, 251.

[33]Simon, "The Explosive Growth of Gambling," 13.

[34]"Casino Failures, Low Profits Sober Some in Gaming Industry," *Louisville (Ky.) Courier-Journal,* January 26, 1996, B4.

[35]Todd Murphy, "Lottery Revenue Is Unlikely to Grow" *Louisville (Ky.) Courier-Journal,* January 26, 1996, B1, 5.

[36]Ibid.

[37]"Gambling Losing Ground," 7.

[38]Simon, "The Explosive Growth of Gambling," 12.

[39]Goodman, *The Luck Business,* 135.

[40]Ibid., 146.

[41]"Gambling Losing Ground," 7.

[42]Goodman, *The Luck Business,* 53.

[43]Simon, "The Explosive Growth of Gambling," 13.

[44]Ibid.

[45]John Landrum, telephone interview with author, February 14, 1996.

[46]"The Lure of Las Vegas," *Congressional Quarterly Researcher,* March 18, 1994, 245.

[47]Simon, "The Explosive Growth of Gambling," 12.

[48]Wayne E. Oates, *Luck: A Secular Faith* (Louisville: Westminster John Knox Press, 1995), xiii.

[49]Ibid., 73.

[50]Ibid., 69–71.

[51]Simon, "The Explosive Growth of Gambling," 12.

[52]Goodman, *The Luck Business,* 38–39.

[53]Ibid., 82.

[54]"Gambling Losing Ground," 1.

[55]David Anderson, "Left and Right Unite to Fight Gambling," *Louisville (Ky.) Western Recorder,* January 23, 1996.

[56]Bill Miller, telephone interview with author.

[57]Oates, *Luck: A Secular Faith,* 88.

[58]Ibid.

[59]Ibid., 102.

Epilogue

Many years ago I read a story about four people who were eating their Sunday dinner at one of their city's finest restaurants. As they ate the delicious meal, they discussed the sermon their pastor had preached in church that morning.

Then, one of the two women grew silent, focusing her attention on the gleaming window near their table. When the others noticed she had quit the conversation, they too looked to see what had captured her attention.

There, on the other side of the sparkling glass, was the face of a dirty child—a child with face pressed against the glass, mouth open, eyes fixed on the plates of food on the elegantly set restaurant tables.

The four grew quiet, each seemingly lost in thought, as if asking, pondering what to do.

Finally, one person spoke. "I know what we should do," she said. "The answer is easy."

And she got up and closed the drapes.

"Faith and works,
works and faith,
fit together hand in glove. . . .
'I'm telling the solemn truth: Whenever you did one of these things to someone overlooked or ignored, that was me—you did it to me'"
(James 2:17; Matt. 25:40 *The Message*).

Joyce Sweeney Martin and her husband, Larry, recently returned to live in their native Kentucky after spending 20 years ministering through the Southern Baptist Home Mission Board in Detroit, Boston, and Atlanta. A graduate of the Southern Baptist Theological Seminary in Louisville, Kentucky, she has been an adjunct professor of Christian education at Gordon Conwell Theological Seminary in South Hamilton, Massachusetts, and at the Northeastern Baptist School of Ministry in Boston, Massachusetts. She is the author of numerous articles and two other books, *You Are My Witness* and *Links to the Past, Designs for the Future: A History of Woman's Missionary Union in New England.*